allergy-free
desserts

allergy-free
desserts

Gluten-free, Dairy-free, Egg-free, Soy-free, and Nut-free Delights

Elizabeth Gordon

Photography by Jason Wyche

WILEY

JOHN WILEY & SONS, INC.

Library of Congress Cataloging-in-Publication Data:

Gordon, Elizabeth, 1976-

Allergy-free desserts / Elizabeth Gordon.

p. cm.

Includes index.

ISBN 978-0-470-44846-5 (cloth)

1. Food allergy—Diet therapy—Recipes. 2. Desserts. I. Title.

RC596.G664 2009

641.5′6318—dc22

2009007117

Printed in China

10 9 8 7 6 5 4 3 2

To Margot and Colombe

contents

This book never would have been possible without the help and support of some of the most cherished people in my life. I owe so much to my husband, Jesse, who tasted and tested almost all of the recipes even from their earliest, most rudimentary, and sometimes yuckiest stages. He was quite a sport. Colombe and Margot, my children, sacrificed much time with me so that I could make this dream a reality. Carmen always cleaned up after me without a single complaint. Chris Pavone and Talia Cohen were instrumental in not only getting the book to publication but in taking care of me along the way. They answered countless questions and gave invaluable advice. I owe a tremendous debt of gratitude to Sarah Montague Oxman who planted the seed of this cookbook in my head and pushed me so hard from the very start. Anne McEniry and Cornelia Tinkler were fantastically dedicated, thorough testers and note takers, even going so far as to take the finished products to their friends for unbiased taste testing. I am forever in their debt, especially since Anne and Cornelia did the work for nothing more than a thank you and the satisfaction of knowing they had done a good deed. Melani Bauman single-handedly revolutionized my cookie decorating and for that I am forever grateful. Justin Schwartz, my editor, was so patient with me and edited this book into exactly what I'd always imagined. Jason Wyche, Leslie Siegel, and Brian Preston-Campbell worked together to make the photography magical. Lucy Barnes offered undying encouragement and support. And of course, I owe so much to my loyal clients. Without their ongoing support and notes of thanks and encouragement, I never would have had the courage to see this through.

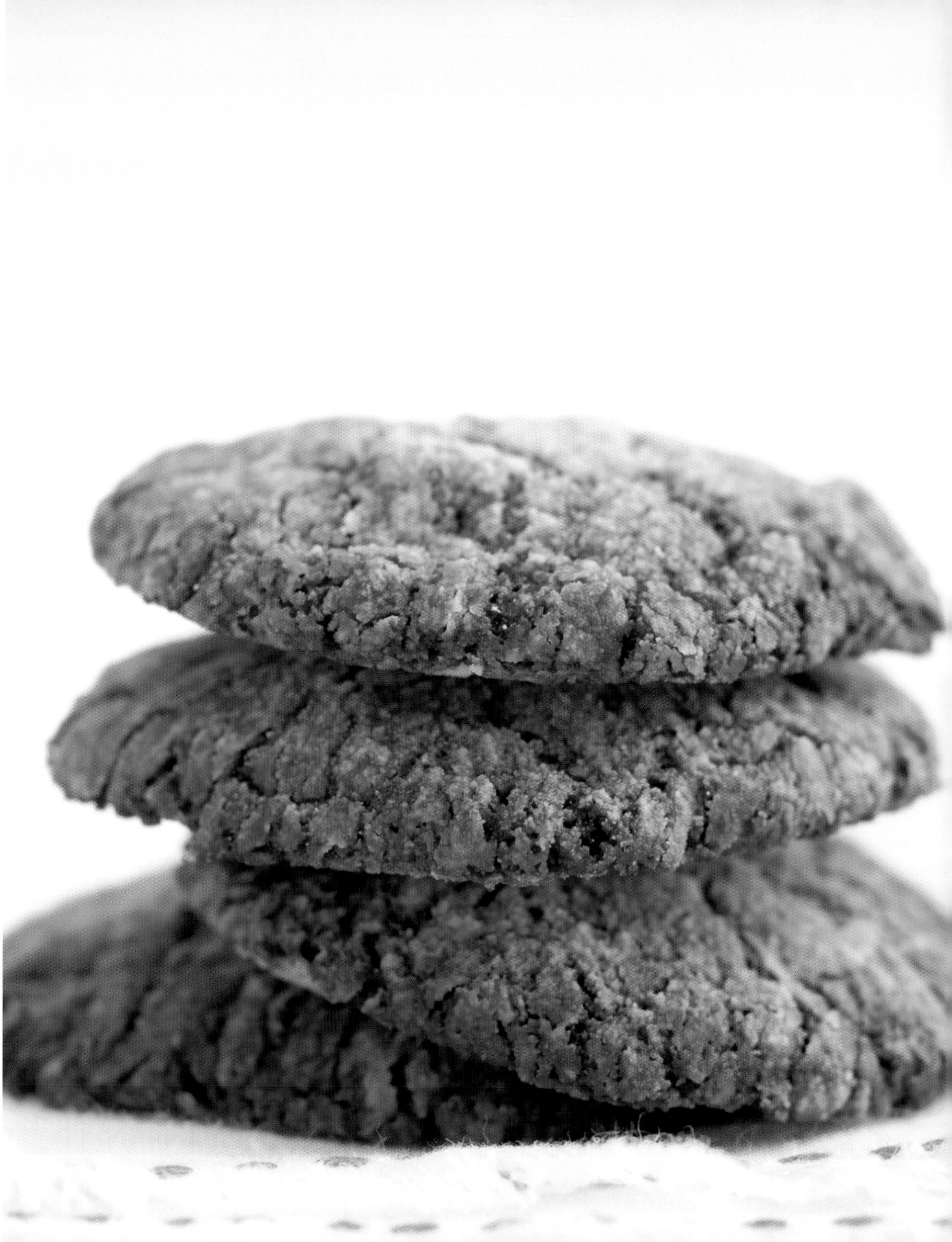

When I was a little girl, I dreamed of two things: baking

professionally and having a family. My mother grew up in her father's restaurant, and she always warned of the crazy hours, the back-breaking labor, the sweltering kitchen, and the cranky mood that inevitably consumes the average restaurateur. Daunted by this lifestyle, I shied away from professional baking to pursue a helping profession, but continued to bake at home and dream of owning a bakery.

And then at twenty-seven, I found myself diagnosed with food allergies and desperate to indulge my sweet tooth. It was at the same time that, on a whim, I decided to intern for a wedding cake designer in my spare time. I loved interning for her, but even inhaling the wheat particles in the bakery air made me itchy and miserable. Discouraged, but not completely disheartened, I considered making treats for people like myself. Since my diagnosis of a wheat and egg allergy, I had virtually forsaken baked goods made without wheat and eggs, finding that everything on the market tasted like sawdust. Though my palate had adapted, I remembered the flavor and texture of buttery, English shortbread cookies and tender, Southern blueberry muffins made with buttermilk. But most of all, I could virtually taste my mother's chocolate chip cookies and homemade birthday cakes slathered with vanilla buttercream.

And then it came to me. Combining the regional influences of the places where I had either grown up or spent a significant amount of time (the Midwest, the South, and Europe), I immediately set to work in my kitchen to create cakes and cookies that tasted just like what I grew up eating but that didn't make me sick. When I finally stumbled upon a recipe that even my nonallergic friends would not only eat with gusto, but that they thought was just a plain old cookie, I knew that I had finally found my calling.

In the midst of my compulsive experimentation, my mother drove out from Ohio to bring my girls some of my childhood mementos, one of which was my little toy kitchen. When she arrived, we talked about the hours that I spent pretending to bake and how I was never alone in my kitchen—my imaginary friend Claude was always there to keep me company and to assist in my adventures.

Just like that, my company was born. Betsy was my nickname when I was a little girl, and Claude was the inspiration behind every mud pie that I ever made. It seemed unfair to leave him out of my real bakery. My baking reminds me of my childhood, of being home and of simpler times. I hope that these recipes will inspire and comfort you the way that they do me.

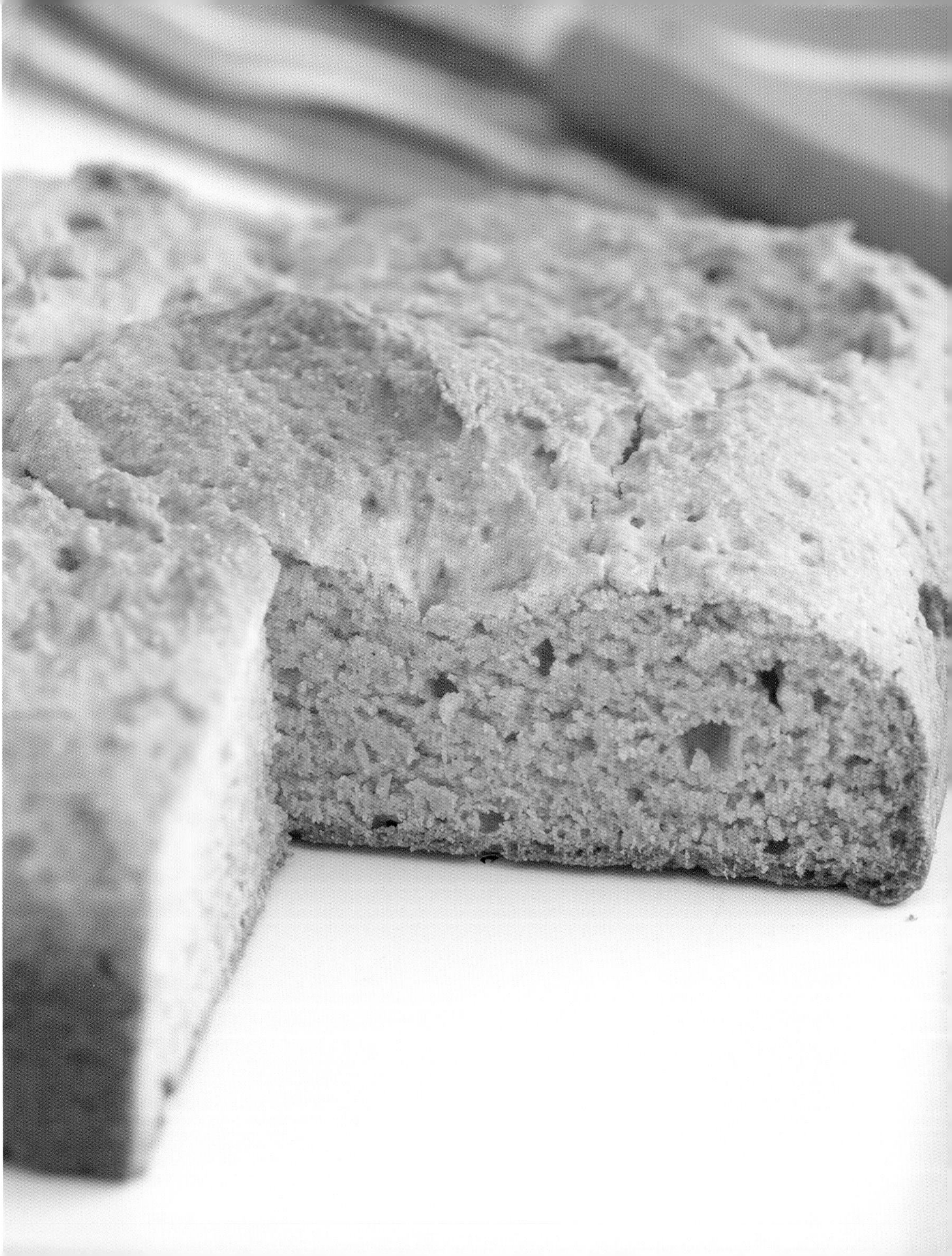

Welcome to allergen-free baking 101!

Baking without all of the traditional ingredients may seem daunting to even the most seasoned baker, and many of the ingredients that I use may sound completely foreign. In fact, you may never have heard of any of them, but I will help you track them down and learn how to use them. I know that I hadn't heard of them until I became completely determined to make desserts that I could and would eat. In the following pages, I will introduce you to the ingredients, what they do and how to use them. Then, I will give you some useful tips that I have learned either working in a bakery, watching my mother in her kitchen, or in professional cake decorating classes that I have taken. All of these tips are so simple, yet they make baking so much easier. Most importantly, have a great time learning this new skill and know that sometimes different is good. Pie crusts aren't as temperamental. There is no such thing as overbeating cake batter and getting a tough cake because there is no gluten in these cake recipes. So, different yes, but in lots of ways better. I promise!

a lexicon of gluten- and
allergy-free baking

Gluten-free—This can be confusing to someone who doesn't suffer from celiac disease or doesn't have a wheat or gluten allergy. When shopping, find products that either say that they are specifically gluten-free, or those that do not contain wheat, rye, barley, malt, triticale, or modified food starch. Modified corn starch is fine, but make sure that the label specifically denotes corn over "food" starch. Modified food starch is generally made from wheat.

Garbanzo Bean Flour—Garbanzo bean flour is obviously made from the garbanzo bean, which is also commonly called the chickpea. It is creamy and not as dry as rice flour, lending a better texture to both cakes and cookies. However, it tastes terrible before it is baked, so I recommend not tasting the batter in any of these recipes.

Potato Starch—Potato starch is often used as a thickener in many sauces and gravies, but in gluten-free baking, it is essential for creating a delicate crumb in cookies and cakes.

Tapioca Flour—Also known as tapioca starch, this is a very finely ground flour made from the tapioca plant. It is very useful in this kind of baking because it lends a slightly sweet flavor, and it helps the baked good bake to a golden brown. Tapioca flour also helps with the texture of the cake or cookie, as it gives cake an appealing spongy texture.

Xanthan Gum—Used to make baked goods rise in the absence of gluten, xanthan gum is the number one most important ingredient in all gluten-free baking. It is made from a microorganism called Xanthomonas campestris that feeds on either corn or soybean plants. If you are allergic to corn or soy, make sure you know where your xanthan gum came from.

Flaxseed Meal—High in fiber and omega-3 fatty acids, ground flaxseeds make an excellent egg substitute. When the ground seeds are mixed with water, the mixture becomes thick and viscous, much like the consistency of an egg white. The flaxseed can lend a slightly nutty flavor, but most of the time, the substitution is flavorless and helps to create the perfect texture for cakes and cookies.

Agar—This is a dried seaweed that is often used as a kosher, vegetarian alternative to gelatin. I use it in several recipes as a thickener and as an egg substitute. It is readily available at most health food stores. However, do not try to substitute it in my recipes that call for gelatin. After many frustrated attempts, I discovered that it doesn't whip to form marshmallow the way that gelatin does.

Lyle's Golden Syrup—I had never heard of this corn syrup alternative until one of my English friends mentioned that she had used it in a frosting. Curiosity piqued, I pressed her for more information and learned that Lyle's is a thick syrup that is easily substituted for high fructose corn syrup. Although Lyle's is still sugar, it is nothing but 100% sugar, not processed fructose. (Some research suggests that fructose is more easily converted to fat by the liver than sucrose and that fructose has been linked to diseases such as diabetes and high cholesterol in animals.) Lyle's is available online and at specialty gourmet food stores. Just know that using Lyle's will make frostings slightly off-white.

Cider Vinegar—Baking soda does its job through a complicated chemical process that is too boring to go into in detail in this book. However, the bottom line is that the process cannot be activated in the absence of something acidic. In most cake recipes, buttermilk or yogurt is used to this end; however, I can't use either of those ingredients in my baking. A little cider vinegar mixed with rice milk provides an adequate substitute for buttermilk, allowing the cake to rise nicely. I thought that it seemed a little strange at first, but it works, and so little vinegar is used that it doesn't affect the flavor of the cake.

Gluten-free Rice Milk—With our new national awareness about celiac disease and gluten intolerance, many rice milks are now stamped with a "gluten-free" seal. However, if your favorite brand is not, or you are baking for a loved one with celiac disease, make sure the rice milk does not contain any barley or malt. If you are still concerned, do not hesitate to phone the manufacturer and ask.

Organic Palm Fruit Oil—I was very concerned about using tropical oils when I first began this endeavor. While tropical oils have gotten a bad rap in the past, new research has revealed that these oils, such as coconut and palm fruit oil, provide health benefits. I recommend using palm fruit oil shortening and coconut oil throughout this cookbook, but I use the different oils for different reasons. The palm fruit oil shortening is the same consistency and yields the same results as a traditional, soy-based shortening. However, there is no soy in this shortening. It is all natural and completely non-hydrogenated.

Organic, Refined Coconut Oil—Coconut oil has very unique properties, and I like to use it under different circumstances than the organic palm oil shortening. Coconut oil has a very low melting point, which means that it is completely liquid at room temperature and solid when chilled. In general, the recipes in this book use liquefied coconut oil, not solid. Because of coconut oil's very low melting point, it doesn't lend the appropriate structure to cookies or cake, and it can be tricky in frostings. Although I offer up one recipe for a coconut oil-based frosting, in general, I prefer not to use it for frostings because coconut oil frostings often turn to liquid once the cake is removed from the refrigerator. However, coconut oil is perfect for making chilled desserts like key lime pie or fudge. The batter can be blended with other ingredients in a blender and then placed in the refrigerator to

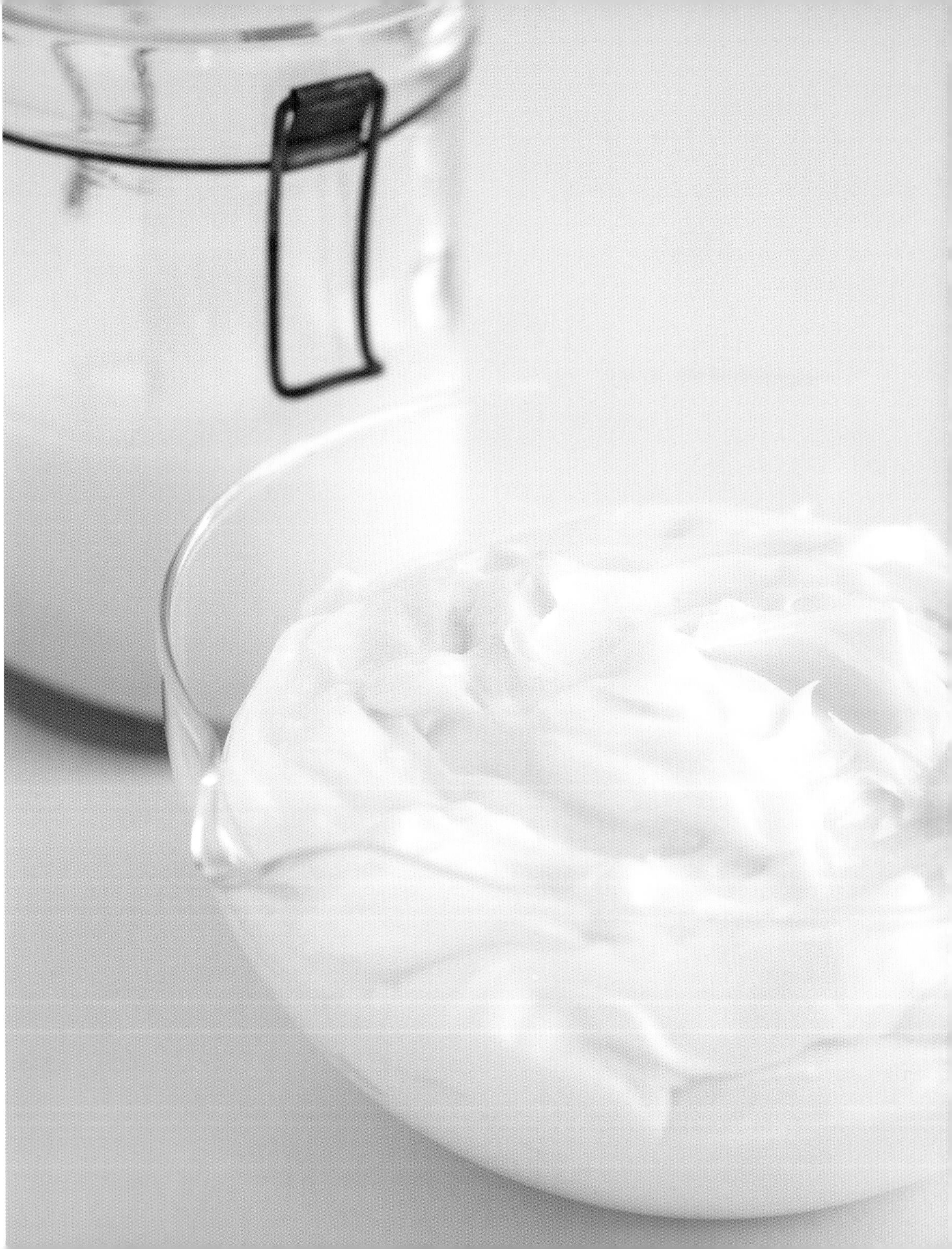

harden to a custardy consistency. Just remember not to leave the finished product out of the refrigerator on a warm day or the dessert will completely melt.

I recommend using organic, refined coconut oil because it is flavorless. Unrefined coconut oil has a very strong flavor that often overpowers a recipe. There is little difference between the two in nutritional value. It is important to note that at present, the FDA has established no guidelines with regard to the term "virgin" as applied to coconut oil. Unlike with olive oil, anyone can claim that their coconut oil is "virgin," meaning that the label means little if anything at all. (See http://www.spectrumorganics.com for more information.)

Granulated and Brown Sugar—Initially, I tested the recipes using natural sugar substitutes like agave, but found that without sugar, I could not build the proper "structure" in the cookies (in other words, they looked like puddles) and the cakes were too dense. Sugar has recently been vilified in the media, but it is a natural substance that I believe is ok to eat, like all other treats, in moderation.

Grade B Maple Syrup—I love to use maple syrup to add depth to chocolate recipes or to impart an unexpected, but delicious flavor to things like pumpkin pie. In researching this book, I discovered that Grade B syrup is just as natural as any other organic brand of maple syrup but that it has a stronger flavor and is a deeper shade of amber, making it ideal for baking and desserts. Grade A syrup is lighter in flavor and color and better suited to pancakes or French toast; however, it is a fine alternative if you cannot find Grade B syrup in your local grocery or health food store. I was recently informed that Grade B syrup is not available in all 50 states as it is not always pasteurized.

Commercially Prepared, Gluten-free, All-purpose Baking Flour—In the cookie recipes, you will notice that I recommend using Bob's Red Mill Gluten Free All-Purpose Baking Flour. I recommend doing so because even though I blend my own mix in the bakery, I use some more obscure flours that are harder to come by in the average health food store or supermarket. Using the commercial blend is a more economical, easier way to achieve the same results as I do at Betsy & Claude Baking Co. If you cannot find Bob's Red Mill in your local grocery store or health food store, it is readily available online and definitely worth the extra work to find. All of the recipes that recommend this particular flour were tested with it. If you absolutely cannot find the Bob's Gluten Free All-Purpose Baking Flour, look for an all-purpose, gluten-free flour that does not contain any baking powder or baking soda and that is made primarily from garbanzo flour. Do not choose one that is rice flour based, as rice flour makes cookies too sandy.

helpful
hints

I feel very lucky to have interned in a bakery and to have grown up in a home where we were constantly rolling out cookie dough or baking a cake. Both experiences have taught me invaluable tricks to make baking easier. From quick cleanup tips to easy release from a baking pan, I have learned some things that you may not have heard of before, but I promise that they will just make baking easier, and therefore, more fun.

You'll note that I have scattered some of these tips and tricks throughout the book to make your baking easier and more fun.

some very smart
cookies

Of course, since cookies are my specialty, this section was so fun to create. I could think of endless cookie recipes, but at Betsy & Claude, I can only do so many flavors. Thus, coming up with these really let me spread my wings and create all kinds of goodies.

Since my allergies appeared as an adult, I was lucky enough to eat cookies and desserts on a near daily basis throughout my younger years. I started my company because I hated the idea of children being deprived of the simple pleasures in life like crispy or chewy cookies loaded with chocolate or dried fruit or oozing with jam. And, working on this section, I discovered that the possibility for allergen-free cookies really is endless.

allergy-free **desserts**

mini black and white cookies

- ⅓ cup gluten-free vanilla rice milk
- ½ teaspoon cider vinegar
- 3 tablespoons water
- 1 tablespoon ground flaxseed meal
- 1¼ cups Betsy's Baking Mix (see page 88)
- 1 teaspoon xanthan gum
- ½ teaspoon baking soda
- ½ teaspoon salt
- ½ cup granulated sugar
- ⅓ cup organic palm fruit oil shortening
- 1 teaspoon vanilla extract
- 1 recipe Black and White Icing (recipe follows)

There is almost nothing more New York than these cookies. I'd never heard of them until I came here, but they are in every deli in the city. A cross between a cake and a cookie, these little cookies are addictive.

Makes about 20 small cookies

Preheat the oven to 350°F. Line 2 baking sheets with parchment paper.

In a cup or small bowl, make "buttermilk" by combining the rice milk and cider vinegar. In another small bowl, combine the water and flaxseed meal and allow to thicken for 3 to 5 minutes. In a medium bowl, whisk together the baking mix, xanthan gum, baking soda, and salt.

In the bowl of a stand mixer, cream together the sugar and shortening until light and fluffy. Scrape down the sides of the bowl, then beat in the flaxseed mixture and vanilla extract. With the mixer on low, alternately add the dry ingredients and the "buttermilk" mixture, starting and ending with the dry ingredients; mix until it is smooth.

Scoop the dough with a small ice cream scoop onto the prepared baking sheets. Bake the cookies for 15 to 17 minutes, or until the cookies are golden and the tops are puffy. The cookies will also spring back when they are touched. Transfer the baking sheets from the oven to cooling racks and cool for 10 minutes, then transfer the cookies directly onto the racks to cool completely. When completely cooled, frost half of the flat side of each cookie with the white (vanilla) icing and half with the black (chocolate) icing.

Store the cookies in an airtight container at room temperature for up to 5 days.

black and white icing

1½ cups confectioners' sugar, sifted
1 tablespoon Lyle's Golden Syrup
¼ teaspoon vanilla extract
4 tablespoons water
2 tablespoons unsweetened cocoa powder

This can be used to frost my Mini Black and White Cookies or to pipe borders on cut-out cookies (then thin it out slightly to make a flood icing to fill in the borders). I suggest using Lyle's Golden Syrup (available at most supermarkets and specialty stores) over corn syrup for this icing, but it will produce a slightly off-white color. If you are making something that requires a true white, feel free to use corn syrup instead.

Makes about 20 small cookies

In a small bowl, mix together the sugar, Golden Syrup, and vanilla. Add in 2 tablespoons of the water and stir until the icing is smooth. If the icing seems too thin to spread on the cookies, add a bit more sugar. If it seems too thick, add a little more water.

Divide the icing into two batches. To make black (chocolate) icing, add the 2 tablespoons of cocoa powder to one of the batches of icing. Add the remaining 2 tablespoons of water to the chocolate icing one teaspoon at a time or until it reaches spreading consistency.

Store the icings, covered with plastic wrap pressed directly to the frosting to prevent dying, and refrigerated, for up to 1 week.

helpful tip: To keep these icings from drying out when not in use, store them in an airtight container with a piece of plastic wrap pressed directly on top. Keep the icing covered whenever you are not working with it.

how to tell when
cookies are done:

In the recipes for cookies, I often suggest that the centers of the cookies should not be "wet," as an indication of doneness. When a cookie is ready to come out of the oven, the edges should be ever so slightly golden and, when lightly touched, the centers should feel neither goopy nor leave a deep indentation.

chocolate crinkle cookies

6 tablespoons water
2 tablespoons ground flaxseed meal
1½ cups Bob's Red Mill Gluten Free All-Purpose Baking Flour
²⁄₃ cup unsweetened cocoa powder
1 teaspoon baking powder
1 teaspoon baking soda
1 teaspoon salt
1 teaspoon xanthan gum
1 cup organic palm fruit oil shortening
¾ cup packed dark brown sugar
¾ cup granulated sugar
1 teaspoon vanilla extract
½ cup confectioners' sugar, sifted

These are so rich, soft, and delicious, they are almost like brownies. Do not be alarmed if you peek into the oven and see them cracking. Those cracks are normal and look quite attractive when the cookies have cooled.

Makes about 2 dozen cookies

Preheat the oven to 350°F and line 2 baking sheets with parchment paper.

In a small bowl, combine the water and flaxseed meal and allow to thicken for 3 to 5 minutes. In a large bowl, whisk together the flour, cocoa, baking powder, baking soda, salt, and xanthan gum.

In the bowl of a stand mixer, cream together the shortening, brown sugar, and granulated sugar. Scrape down the sides of the bowl, add in the vanilla and the flaxseed meal mixture, and beat until it is fluffy and the flaxseed is thoroughly mixed in. Add in the flour mixture and mix the batter until thoroughly combined.

Drop rounded tablespoonfuls of the dough into the confectioners' sugar, rolling the cookies around to form balls. Place the balls 2 inches apart, to allow for spreading, on the prepared baking sheets. Bake for 14 minutes or until the tops of the cookies no longer look wet. Transfer the baking sheets from the oven to cooling racks and cool for 10 minutes, then transfer the cookies directly onto the racks to cool completely.

Store the cookies in an airtight container at room temperature for up to 5 days, or freeze for up to 3 months.

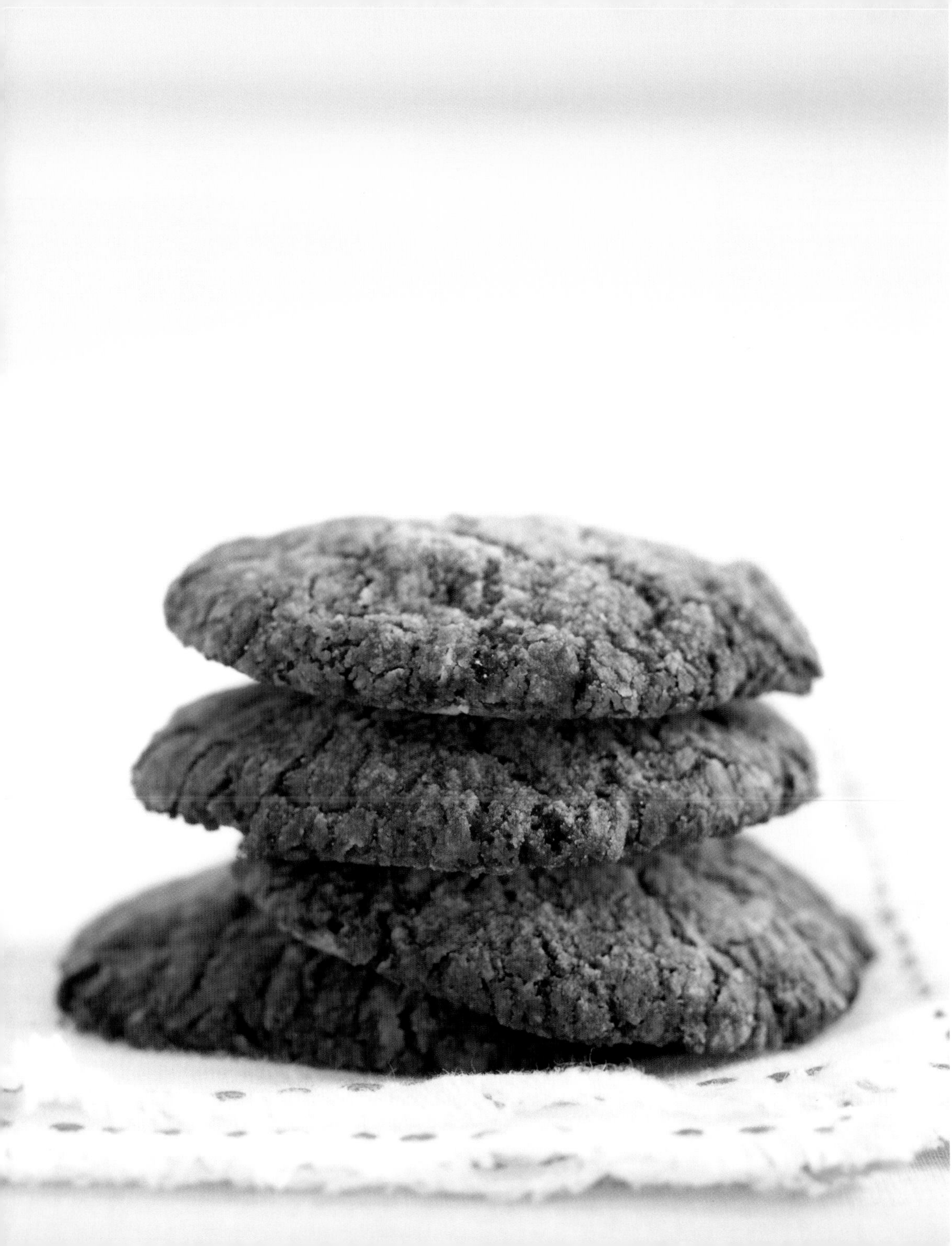

chewy molasses crinkles

6 tablespoons water
1 tablespoon ground
  flaxseed meal
2¼ cups Bob's Red Mill Gluten
  Free All-Purpose Baking
  Flour
2 teaspoons baking soda
1¼ teaspoons ground ginger
1 teaspoon ground cinnamon
1 teaspoon xanthan gum
½ teaspoon ground cloves
¼ teaspoon salt
1 cup packed dark brown
  sugar
¾ cup organic palm fruit oil
  shortening
¼ cup molasses

I can remember bursting through the back door of our house after school in the second grade to be greeted by a plate of molasses crinkles and a note that my mother was at my grandparents' picking cherries. I don't think I could dream up a more Midwestern moment if I tried.

Makes about 2 dozen cookies

Preheat the oven to 375°F and line 2 baking sheets with parchment paper.

In a small bowl, combine the water and flaxseed meal and allow to thicken for 3 to 5 minutes. In a large bowl, whisk together the flour, baking soda, ginger, cinnamon, xanthan gum, cloves, and salt.

In the bowl of a stand mixer, cream the brown sugar and shortening until they are fluffy. Scrape down the sides of the bowl and add in the molasses. Beat the batter until it is fluffy again and scrape down the sides again. Pour in the flaxseed meal mixture and beat the batter until thoroughly combined. Pour the dry ingredients into the batter and mix in until thoroughly combined.

Drop the cookies onto the prepared baking sheets by heaping tablespoonfuls or with a small ice cream scoop to make the cookies uniform. Bake for 8 minutes, or until the centers no longer look wet. Transfer the baking sheets from the oven to cooling racks and cool for 10 minutes, then transfer the cookies directly onto the racks to cool completely.

Store the cookies in an airtight container at room temperature for up to 5 days, or freeze for up to 3 months.

haystacks

1¾ cups granulated sugar
½ cup gluten-free vanilla rice milk
¼ cup organic refined coconut oil (stir before measuring if not completely liquid)
¼ cup unsweetened cocoa powder
2 cups gluten-free rolled oats
½ cup smooth or crunchy sunflower seed butter
1 teaspoon vanilla extract

Haystacks are so fun to make with kids since they never go into the oven. Even though they were a lunchbox staple when I was growing up, these need to be refrigerated until just before serving.

Makes about 3 dozen cookies

Line 2 baking sheets with parchment paper.

In a medium saucepan, combine the sugar, rice milk, coconut oil, and cocoa powder. Heat over medium heat, stirring frequently, until the mixture comes to a boil, then boil the mixture, stirring constantly, for exactly 1½ minutes, but no longer. Remove the pan from the heat.

Stir in the oats, sunflower seed butter, and vanilla. Scoop the mixture onto the prepared baking sheets by tablespoonfuls and refrigerate until the cookies are hardened.

These cookies should be refrigerated until just before serving due to the low melting point of the coconut oil. They may be frozen in an airtight container for up to 3 months..

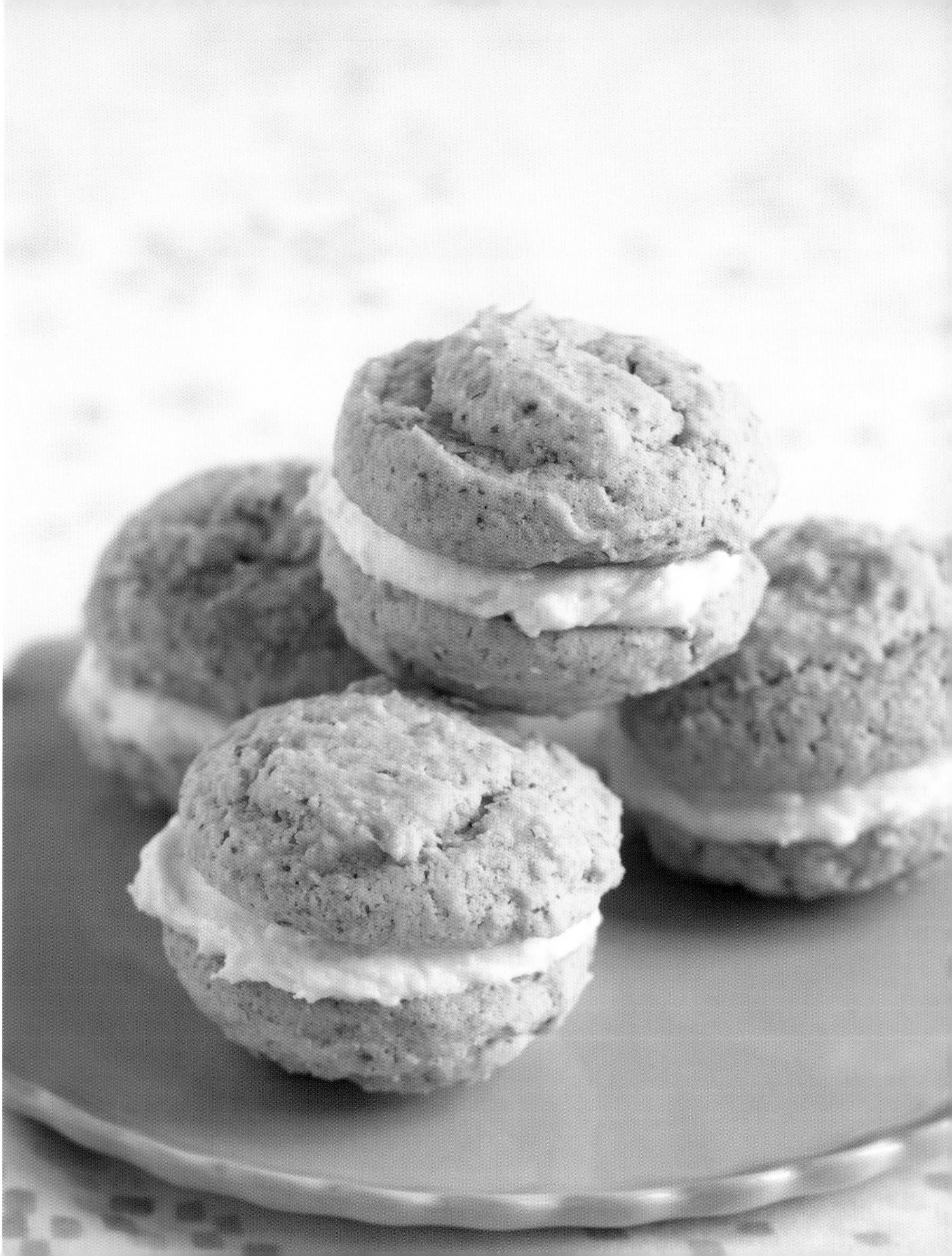

lemon sugar cookies

6 tablespoons water
2 tablespoons ground flaxseed meal
2¼ cups Bob's Red Mill Gluten Free All-Purpose Baking Flour
1 teaspoon baking powder
1 teaspoon baking soda
1 teaspoon xanthan gum
¼ teaspoon salt
1 cup organic palm fruit oil shortening
¾ cup granulated sugar
¾ cup packed light brown sugar
1 tablespoon lemon extract Grated zest from 1 large lemon

These are great companions to a picnic lunch. They are refreshing and chewy and always delicious when they are sandwiched with my Vanilla Buttercream Frosting (see page 93).

Makes about 2 dozen cookies or 1 dozen sandwiches

Preheat the oven to 350°F and line 2 baking sheets with parchment paper.

In a small bowl, combine the water and flaxseed meal and allow to thicken for 3 to 5 minutes. In a large bowl, whisk together the flour, baking powder, baking soda, xanthan gum, and salt.

In the bowl of a stand mixer, cream together the shortening and sugars. Scrape down the sides of the bowl, add in the lemon extract, lemon zest, and the flaxseed meal mixture, and beat the batter again until it is fluffy and the flaxseed is thoroughly mixed in. Add in the dry ingredients and mix the batter until the dry ingredients are thoroughly combined.

Using a small ice cream scoop, drop the dough 2 inches apart onto the prepared baking sheets. Bake for 14 minutes, or until the centers are no longer wet. Transfer the baking sheets from the oven to cooling racks and cool for 10 minutes, then transfer the cookies directly onto the racks to cool completely. Store the cookies in an airtight container at room temperature for up to 5 days, or freeze for up to 3 months.

raspberry-cardamom sandwich cookies

3 cups Bob's Red Mill Gluten Free All-Purpose Baking Flour

1½ cups granulated sugar

1 tablespoon baking powder

1½ teaspoons salt

1 teaspoon xanthan gum

¼ teaspoon ground allspice

¼ teaspoon ground cardamom

1 cup organic palm fruit oil shortening

½ cup gluten-free rice milk

¾ cup raspberry jam

My mother makes a bar version of these cookies every Christmas. She doesn't remember where she got the recipe, but I suspect it was from the years that she and my father spent living in Europe.

Makes about 18 sandwich cookies

Preheat the oven to 375°F and line 2 baking sheets with parchment paper.

In the bowl of a stand mixer, whisk together the flour, sugar, baking powder, salt, xanthan gum, allspice, and cardamom. Cut in the shortening with a pastry cutter until a coarse meal forms. Place the bowl in the mixer, attach the paddle, and begin mixing on low speed. With the mixer running, pour in the rice milk until a dough forms.

Drop the dough by tablespoonfuls onto the prepared baking sheets, leaving about 1 inch between each cookie. Then, flatten them with the bottom of a glass. Bake the cookies for 12 to 14 minutes, or until the edges of the cookies are golden brown and the centers are no longer wet. Transfer the baking sheets from the oven to cooling racks and cool for 10 minutes, then transfer the cookies directly onto the racks to cool completely. When the cookies are completely cool, make "sandwiches" by spreading the bottom of 1 cookie with 1 teaspoon of the jam and placing the bottom of another cookie on top.

Store the sandwich cookies in an airtight container at room temperature for up to 5 days.

using an ice cream scoop for uniform
cookie size:

This is the best way to make sure that you end up with uniform cookies, and using an ice cream scoop also makes the cookies look more professional. I like to use a $1\frac{1}{2}$-inch diameter ice cream scoop to make my cookies. Oftentimes, this size ice cream scoop is labeled as a "cookie scoop" when they are sold in supermarkets and retail houseware stores. However, as there is no hard and fast rule about how large to make a cookie, feel free to use a melon baller for bite-size cookies or a $\frac{1}{2}$ cup ice cream scoop for a jumbo cookie. Just remember to adjust the baking time accordingly.

pretend peanut butter cookies

3 tablespoons water
1 tablespoon ground
   flaxseed meal
1¼ cups Bob's Red Mill Gluten
   Free All-Purpose Baking
   Flour
1 teaspoon baking powder
½ teaspoon salt
½ teaspoon xanthan gum
½ cup organic palm fruit oil
   shortening
½ cup granulated sugar
½ cup packed light brown
   sugar
½ cup sunflower seed butter
½ teaspoon vanilla extract

Those who have tasted these swear that they really taste just like peanut butter cookies. They look like them, too. The only difference is that they aren't.

Makes about 20 small cookies

Preheat the oven to 375°F and line 2 baking sheets with parchment paper.

In a cup or small bowl, combine the water and flaxseed meal and allow to thicken for 3 to 5 minutes. In large bowl, whisk together the flour, baking powder, salt, and xanthan gum.

In the bowl of a stand mixer, cream together the shortening, sugars, and sunflower seed butter. Scrape down the sides of the bowl, then beat in the flaxseed mixture and the vanilla. Scrape down the sides of the bowl again. Stir in the dry ingredients until thoroughly combined.

Using a small ice cream scoop, drop the dough 2 inches apart onto the prepared sheets. Press the cookies down with the tines of a fork (dipped in sugar) in the criss-cross pattern characteristic of peanut butter cookies.

Bake the cookies for 10 to 12 minutes or until the edges are golden and the tops no longer look wet. Transfer the baking sheets from the oven to cooling racks and cool for 10 minutes, then transfer the cookies directly onto the racks to cool completely.

Store the cookies in an airtight container at room temperature for up to 5 days, or freeze for up to 3 months.

some very smart **cookies**

chocolate shortbread cut-out cookies

2 ounces organic unsweetened baking chocolate, chopped
3 tablespoons water
1 tablespoon ground flaxseed meal
3 cups Bob's Red Mill Gluten Free All-Purpose Baking Flour
1 teaspoon xanthan gum
$3/4$ teaspoon baking powder
$1/4$ teaspoon salt
1 cup granulated sugar
1 cup organic palm fruit oil shortening
3 tablespoons plus 1 teaspoon gluten-free vanilla rice milk
  Decorating Icing (recipe follows)

With this recipe you can create the most adorable shapes, then decorate them just as beautifully as they are at your local bakery. I find they make an easy, economical, and heart-felt holiday gift, and as they are free of gluten, dairy, soy, nut, and egg, everyone can enjoy them together.

Makes 4 dozen $3^1/_2$-inch cookies

Preheat the oven to 375°F and line 2 baking sheets with parchment paper.

Place the chocolate in a microwaveable bowl and melt the chocolate in the microwave for about 45 seconds. Stir after 20 seconds, making sure it doesn't scorch. Stir the chocolate until it is smooth and set it aside to cool.

In a small bowl, combine the water and flaxseed meal and allow to thicken for 3 to 5 minutes. In a large bowl, whisk together the flour, xanthan gum, baking powder, and salt.

In the bowl of a stand mixer, cream together the sugar and shortening. Scrape down the sides of the bowl, add in the flaxseed meal mixture and the melted chocolate, and beat again until fluffy and the flaxseed is thoroughly mixed in. Scrape down the sides again.

chocolate shortbread cut-out cookies

Add in the dry ingredients and mix the batter until the dry ingredients are thoroughly combined; the dough will be coarse. Stir in the rice milk, then mix until the dough begins to come together. Remove the bowl from the mixer and, using your hands, form the dough into a ball. Divide the dough in half and wrap one half in plastic wrap.

Roll out the remaining half of the dough between 2 sheets of parchment paper until it is $1/4$ inch thick and cut it into the desired shapes. Place on the prepared baking sheet and bake for 10 minutes. Repeat the rolling out, cutting, and baking of the dough until all of the dough has been used. Transfer the baking sheets from the oven to cooling racks and cool for 10 minutes, then transfer the cookies directly onto the racks to cool completely. Decorate with the icing.

Store the decorated cookies in an airtight container at room temperature for up to 3 days. Undecorated cookies may be frozen in an airtight container for up to 3 months.

note: Alternatively, the cookies may be brushed with a drop of water and sprinkled with colored sugar or sprinkles before baking, or they may be decorated with Vanilla Buttercream Frosting (see page 93) and sprinkles after they have cooled.

how to decorate
cut-out cookies

When I decorate my cut-out cookies, I generally use pastry bags fitted with a #2 tip to outline the design and then flood the inside of the outline with flood icing in a pastry bag fitted with a #4 tip. If you have experience using a pastry bag and tips, then this is an easy way to decorate. However, if you are working with children or feel a little intimidated by tips and bags, then I recommend using plastic decorating squeeze bottles. It's a really easy way to achieve the same effect, and it can be a lot neater as well as easier to clean up. These bottles are easily found at most craft stores or online (www.coppergifts.com). The holes in the spouts are generally small enough to precisely outline the smallest cookies, but if you need a faster flow, then simply snip the top of the spout to achieve the desired effect.

decorating icing

½ cup confectioners' sugar, sifted
2 teaspoons Lyle's Golden Syrup or corn syrup
2 teaspoons water
1 drop peppermint extract or vanilla extract

This icing is such an easy way to get bakery-quality cookies in no time. Although the yield seems small, it is just enough to fit one of the 2-ounce decorating squeeze bottles that I recommend, and by using smaller batches, you ensure that your icing never dries out. So make just one batch of the icing at a time. It takes only a minute to whip up another batch.

Makes enough to decorate twelve $3\frac{1}{2}$ -inch cookies

In a small bowl, stir together all of the ingredients until they are smooth and spreadable. Pour the icing into decorating squeeze bottles. As desired, draw an outline of icing around the edge of all of the cookies, then, after all of the cookies have been outlined, go back to the beginning and "flood" the middle of the outline with the rest of the icing. This allows the outline to dry just a little before flooding. Make more batches of icing as needed.

allergy-free **desserts**

maple cookies

3 tablespoons water
1 tablespoon ground
   flaxseed meal
1³/₄ cups Bob's Red Mill Gluten
   Free All-Purpose Baking
   Flour
2 teaspoons baking powder
¹/₂ teaspoon xanthan gum
¹/₄ teaspoon salt
1 cup packed light brown
   sugar
¹/₂ cup organic palm fruit oil
   shortening
¹/₂ cup Grade B maple syrup
¹/₂ teaspoon vanilla extract
¹/₂ cup sweetened flaked
   coconut

These cookies are chewy and delicious. In fact, they are so good that when set in front a group of teenagers, they were gobbled up in minutes.

Makes about 2 dozen cookies

Preheat the oven to 375°F and line 2 baking sheets with parchment paper.

In a small bowl, combine the water and flaxseed meal and allow to thicken for 3 to 5 minutes. In a large bowl, whisk together the flour, baking powder, xanthan gum, and salt.

In the bowl of a stand mixer, cream together the sugar and shortening. Scrape down the sides of the bowl, add in the flaxseed meal mixture and beat the batter again until it is fluffy and the flaxseed is thoroughly mixed in. Scrape down the sides of the bowl and beat in the maple syrup and vanilla. Add in the dry ingredients and mix the batter until thoroughly combined. Fold in the coconut.

Using a small ice cream scoop, drop the dough 2 inches apart onto the prepared baking sheets. Bake for 10 to 12 minutes, or until the centers no longer appear wet. Transfer the baking sheets from the oven to cooling racks and cool for 10 minutes, then transfer the cookies directly onto the racks to cool completely.

frozen coconut macaroon bonbons

2²/₃ cups (one 7-ounce bag) sweetened flaked coconut
¹/₄ cup well-shaken, unsweetened coconut milk (not light)
2 tablespoons liquefied organic refined coconut oil (stir before measuring if not completely liquid)
1 tablespoon agave syrup
¹/₂ teaspoon vanilla extract
¹/₄ teaspoon salt
¹/₂ cup gluten-, soy-, dairy-, egg-, and nut-free semisweet chocolate chips, melted and cooled

These are delicious alone or dipped in melted, semisweet chocolate. They are super quick and easy to whip up, and everyone always loves them. Given their flavor and size, they remind me of little, creamy, poppable bonbons. Make sure to keep them frozen until just before serving, as the coconut oil will cause them to melt at room temperature.

Makes about 16 bonbons

Line a baking sheet with parchment paper.

In a large mixing bowl, stir together the coconut, coconut milk, oil, agave syrup, vanilla, and salt. Drop by tablespoonfuls onto the prepared baking sheet, roll into balls, and freeze for at least 1 hour.

Remove the bonbons from the freezer and dip the bottoms into the cooled melted chocolate. Return the bonbons to the freezer for at least 20 minutes, or until ready to serve.

Store the completely hardened bonbons in an airtight container and keep frozen for up to 2 weeks.

"Always measure

coconut

oil in its liquid form and organic palm fruit oil in its solid form."

thumbprint gems

3 tablespoons water
1 tablespoon ground
  flaxseed meal
2¼ cups Bob's Red Mill Gluten
  Free All-Purpose Baking
  Flour
1½ teaspoons ground
  cinnamon
1 teaspoon baking soda
1 teaspoon baking powder
1 teaspoon salt
1 teaspoon xanthan gum
½ teaspoon ground nutmeg
¼ teaspoon ground allspice
¼ teaspoon ground cloves
1 cup organic palm fruit oil
  shortening
¾ cup packed dark brown
  sugar
¾ cup granulated sugar
1 teaspoon vanilla extract
½– ¾ cup apricot or
  strawberry jam

The first time that I made thumbprint cookies, I was twelve years old, and I needed a project to do with the kids I was babysitting. They went over very well, not only because they were so yummy, but also because the kids loved to push the indentation into the center before we filled them with jam and put them in the oven.

Makes about 50 cookies

Preheat the oven to 350°F and line 2 baking sheets with parchment paper.

In a small bowl, combine the water and flaxseed meal and allow to thicken for 3 to 5 minutes. In a large mixing bowl, combine the flour, cinnamon, baking soda, baking powder, salt, xanthan gum, nutmeg, allspice, and cloves.

In the bowl of a stand mixer, cream together the shortening and sugars. Scrape down the sides of the bowl, add in the flaxseed meal mixture, and beat again until the batter is fluffy and the flaxseed is thoroughly mixed in. Scrape down the sides of the bowl and beat in the vanilla. Add in the dry ingredients and mix until thoroughly combined. The dough will be coarse.

Using a tablespoon measure, scoop out the dough, press it together, and roll it into a ball. Place the balls 2 inches apart on the prepared baking sheets. Using the tip of your finger or thumb, press a light indentation into the top of each ball and fill with ½ teaspoon of the jam of your choice.

Bake the cookies for 10 to 12 minutes, or until the cookies are golden brown. Transfer the baking sheets from the oven to cooling racks and cool for 10 minutes, then transfer the cookies directly onto the racks to cool completely.

Store the cookies in an airtight container at room temperature for up to 5 days.

helpful tip: If the jam begins to look dry while baking, add an additional ¼ tsp of jam to each cookie five minutes before the end of the baking time.

some very smart **cookies**

bite
off
more
than
you
can
chew

bars

To me, no beach picnic or kid's lunch is complete without a bar cookie. They are more durable than the average drop variety, and they are almost always more decadent. Just a tiny piece usually goes a long way toward satisfying a craving for something sweet. Gooey and chewy, even without gluten, dairy, soy, nuts, and eggs, bar cookies are like little squares of manna to perk up anyone's day.

quick cherry crumb bars

Shortbread Crust
- 2 cups Betsy's Baking Mix (see page 88)
- 1 teaspoon xanthan gum
- 1/8 teaspoon salt
- 1/2 cup plus 2 tablespoons organic palm fruit oil shortening
- 1/4 cup granulated sugar
- 1/4 cup packed light brown sugar
- 1 teaspoon vanilla extract

Streusel Topping and Filling
- 1 cup Betsy's Baking Mix (see page 88)
- 1/2 cup packed light brown sugar
- 1/4 teaspoon salt
- 1/4 teaspoon xanthan gum
- 1/2 cup organic palm fruit oil shortening, chilled for 30 minutes before using
- One 21-ounce can gluten-free cherry pie filling

I find inspiration for my recipes everywhere, and the deli is no exception. One day I was standing in line waiting for some lunch and looked down to see cherry bars. They looked so good, so absolutely mouthwatering, that I ran home and created a version for myself.

Makes 9 large bars or 12 smaller bars

Preheat the oven to 350°F.

To make the crust, mix together the baking mix, xanthan gum, and salt in a medium bowl. In the bowl of a stand mixer, cream together the shortening and sugars. Stir in the vanilla. Mix in the dry ingredients until they are thoroughly combined, then press the dough into a 9 x 13-inch baking pan. Chill the crust in the refrigerator for 20 minutes. Remove the crust from the refrigerator and prick it all over with a fork.

Bake the crust for 20 minutes, or until lightly browned. Transfer the baked crust from the oven to a cooling rack and cool for at least 30 minutes. Maintain the oven temperature.

To make the streusel topping, in a medium bowl, whisk together the baking mix, brown sugar, salt, and xanthan gum. With a fork, cut in the shortening so that the mixture is combined but there are still large clumps in the mixture; if the clumps are not present, the streusel topping will just melt into the cherry filling when it is baked. Freeze the crumb topping for at least 30 minutes.

CONTINUED ON PAGE 52

bite off more than you can chew **bars**

quick cherry crumb bars

Spread the cherry filling over the prepared shortbread crust. Sprinkle the streusel topping over the cherry filling, then bake for 35 minutes. Remove from the oven and let cool completely in the pan on a cooling rack before cutting.

Store the bars in an airtight container and refrigerated for up to 3 days.

helpful tip: If you have trouble finding prepared cherry pie filling that isn't gluten-free, you can easily make the filling. Combine 1 pound of thawed, pitted, frozen cherries with $2\frac{3}{4}$ cups of granulated sugar and 2 tablespoons of cornstarch in a large sauté pan. Over medium heat, cook, stirring constantly, for 8 to 10 minutes, or until the cherries begin to release their juice and the mixture thickens. Use the cherry mixture as directed above.

how to zest a lemon
or lime:

Several of the recipes in this book call for a significant amount of citrus zest and citrus juice. There are actual tools referred to as "zesters," and I find mine invaluable in the kitchen. Zesting tools are sold at most home or hardware stores. If you cannot find one, it is just as easy to zest a lemon or lime on a Microplane grater or on the fine side of your average cheese grater; it might just take a little longer than zesting with a zester. When working on a recipe that requires both the zest and the juice of the lemon or lime, make sure to zest the fruit before squeezing the juice.

lemon squares

Shortbread Crust

- 2 cups Betsy's Baking Mix (see page 88)
- 1 teaspoon xanthan gum
- $\frac{1}{8}$ teaspoon salt
- $\frac{1}{2}$ cup plus 2 tablespoons organic palm fruit oil shortening
- $\frac{1}{4}$ cup granulated sugar
- $\frac{1}{4}$ cup packed light brown sugar
- 1 teaspoon vanilla extract

Filling

- 3 cups confectioners' sugar, sifted, plus extra for dusting
- $\frac{1}{2}$ cup cornstarch
- 1 cup water
- 2 packets unflavored gelatin
- $\frac{2}{3}$ cup freshly squeezed lemon juice
- $\frac{1}{4}$ cup packed freshly grated lemon zest

I went to high school in the South, where lemon squares are an essential part of any picnic, barbecue, or tailgate event. So, these were one of the first things that I wanted to recreate when I started playing around with gluten-, dairy-, soy-, nut-, and egg-free recipes.

Makes about 20 small squares

Preheat the oven to 350°F.

To make the crust, mix together the baking mix, xanthan gum, and salt in a medium bowl. In the bowl of a stand mixer, cream together the shortening and sugars. Stir in the vanilla. Mix in the dry ingredients until they are thoroughly combined, then press the dough into a 9 x 13-inch baking pan. Chill the crust in the refrigerator for 20 minutes. Remove the crust from the refrigerator and prick it all over with a fork.

Bake the crust for 20 minutes, or until lightly browned. Transfer the baked crust from the oven to cooling racks and cool for at least 30 minutes. Maintain the oven temperature.

While the crust is cooling, make the filling. In a medium saucepan, whisk together 3 cups of the confectioners' sugar and the cornstarch. Continue whisking and slowly add the water. Whisking constantly, bring the mixture to a full boil over medium-high heat (8 to 10 minutes). Sprinkle the gelatin over the boiling mixture and stir to dissolve it. Reduce the heat to medium and continue cooking, stirring constantly, for another 5 minutes; the mixture should be quite thick. Remove the custard from the heat and stir in the lemon juice and zest. Pour the lemon custard mixture over the cooled crust.

Bake for 30 minutes. Remove from the oven and let cool completely in the pan on a cooling rack. Dust with confectioners' sugar and cut into squares for serving.

Store the lemon squares in an airtight container and refrigerated for up to 3 days.

bite off more than you can chew **bars**

panda bars

Crust

2 recipes Chocolate Cookie Crust (see page 141), prepared and pressed into a 9 x 13 x 2-inch baking pan

Filling

2 cups prepared Vanilla Buttercream Frosting (see page 93)

One 3.5-ounce can sweetened shredded coconut

Topping

3 ounces gluten-, soy-, dairy-, egg-, and nut-free semisweet chocolate chips

2 ounces unsweetened chocolate, chopped

1 tablespoon organic palm fruit oil shortening

Here is another recipe inspired by Dr. Kennedy, my high school advisor and calculus teacher. He knew his way around a proof, but was even better in the kitchen.

Makes 9 large bars or 12 smaller bars

Chill the prepared chocolate crust in the pan for at least 30 minutes.

Meanwhile, to make the filling, beat together the frosting and coconut. When fluffy and well combined, spread the mixture over the prepared crust. Refrigerate for at least 30 minutes to set.

To make the topping, in the top of a double boiler set over simmering water, melt together the semisweet chocolate, unsweetened chocolate, and shortening, stirring until smooth. Pour the chocolate mixture over the chilled filling, tilting the pan from side to side to spread it evenly. Chill for at least 1 hour, then cut into bars to serve.

Store the bars in an airtight container and refrigerated for up to 3 days.

note: These bars should be chilled until immediately before they are served, due to the low melting point of the coconut oil in the frosting. For easy cutting, use a knife dipped in hot water and then quickly dried to cut the bars.

marshmallow blondies

6 tablespoons water
2 tablespoons ground
   flaxseed meal
1½ cups Bob's Red Mill Gluten
   Free All-Purpose Baking
   Flour
2 teaspoons baking powder
1 teaspoon salt
½ teaspoon xanthan gum
¾ cup Butterscotch Sauce
   (see page 176), slightly
   cooled
⅔ cup packed dark brown
   sugar
1 tablespoon organic
   refined coconut oil
   (stir before measuring if
   not completely liquid)
1½ teaspoons vanilla extract
2 cups gluten- and egg-free
   marshmallows
1 cup gluten-, soy-, dairy-,
   egg-, and nut-free
   semisweet chocolate chips

These are a gooey, gluten-, dairy-, soy-, nut-, and egg-free version of blondie brownies. The inspiration for these came from my high school calculus teacher Dr. Kennedy. He is an amazing baker, and this is my take on one of his best recipes.

Makes 24 bars

Preheat the oven to 350°F and lightly grease a 9 x 13-inch baking pan with canola oil.

In a small bowl, combine the water and flaxseed meal and allow to thicken for 3 to 5 minutes. In a medium mixing bowl, whisk together the flour, baking powder, salt, and xanthan gum. In another bowl, combine the butterscotch sauce, brown sugar, coconut oil, vanilla, and the flaxseed mixture. Stir in the flour mixture until thoroughly combined, then fold in the marshmallows and chocolate chips.

Spread the batter in the prepared pan and bake for 20 minutes. Then turn down the heat to 325°F and bake for another 20 minutes, or until a toothpick inserted in the center comes out clean. Let the blondies cool completely in the pan on a rack before cutting. (I do not like crispy edges, so I prefer to cut off the edges before serving.)

Store the blondies, tightly wrapped and refrigerated, for up to 5 days.

fudgy brownies

3 tablespoons plus $\frac{1}{2}$ cup freshly brewed espresso, cooled
1 tablespoon ground flaxseed meal
1$\frac{3}{4}$ cups Bob's Red Mill Gluten Free All-Purpose Baking Flour
1 cup granulated sugar
$\frac{1}{2}$ cup unsweetened cocoa powder
2$\frac{1}{2}$ teaspoons baking powder
1 teaspoon baking soda
1 teaspoon salt
$\frac{1}{4}$ teaspoon xanthan gum
$\frac{1}{2}$ cup canola oil
1 teaspoon vanilla extract
$\frac{1}{2}$ cup gluten-, soy-, dairy-, egg-, and nut-free semisweet chocolate chips

Brownies feel like a bake sale staple to me. These are fudgy and chewy, and great to pack in a lunch or take to a picnic at the beach.

Makes 16 brownies

Preheat the oven to 350°F and lightly grease a 9-inch round cake pan with canola oil.

In a small bowl, combine 3 tablespoons of the espresso and the flaxseed meal and allow to thicken for 3 to 5 minutes. In another small bowl, whisk together the flour, sugar, cocoa powder, baking powder, baking soda, salt, and xanthan gum. Pour in the canola oil, vanilla, and the remaining $\frac{1}{2}$ cup of espresso. Stir with a wooden spoon until thoroughly combined and smooth. Fold in the chocolate chips.

Pour the batter into the prepared pan and bake for 40 minutes, or until the brownies are firm and a toothpick inserted in the center comes out clean. Let the brownies cool completely in the pan on a rack before cutting them into triangles.

Store the brownies, tightly wrapped and refrigerated, for up to 5 days.

crispy rice squares

1 cup brown rice syrup
1 cup granulated sugar
1¼ teaspoons salt
8 ounces gluten- and egg-free mini marshmallows
1 teaspoon vanilla extract
6 cups gluten-free crisped rice cereal

These are such a staple of childhood that I cannot imagine growing up without them. They graced every single bake-sale table and made it to every potluck dinner. When making these, it's really important to use a gluten-free "crisped" rice cereal. I learned the hard way that puffed rice does not work in this recipe. My daughter specifically asked me to use real cereal the next time.

Makes about 16 bars

In a medium saucepan, combine the rice syrup, sugar, and salt over medium heat, stirring occasionally. Keep a close eye on the rice syrup as it cooks, as it can easily burn. Continue cooking until the mixture is bubbly and the sugar has completely dissolved. Remove it from the heat and stir in the marshmallows and vanilla extract until completely melted and the mixture is smooth.

Pour the syrup mixture over the cereal in a large bowl and combine well with a lightly-oiled spoon (to prevent sticking). Press the mixture with very lightly oiled hands into a greased 9 x 13-inch baking pan. Allow the rice mixture to cool for at least 1 hour before cutting it with a serrated knife into squares.

Store the squares tightly wrapped in an airtight container and at room temperature for up to 3 days.

bite off more than you can chew **bars**

lickety-split
quick
breads

Quick breads were the very first thing our class studied in seventh grade home economics. They are known as "quick" because they require no yeast and, therefore, no rising time. These recipes are among my favorites to eat because many of them are like cake, but they are fine to eat warm. There is no need to wait for these to cool completely because no frosting goes on top. To me, this is the essence of the quick bread. Never mind that they do not contain yeast, it just means they get to my tummy faster than traditional breads!

allergy-free **desserts**

cornbread

1 cup gluten-free vanilla rice milk
1 teaspoon cider vinegar
1 cup Betsy's Baking Mix (see page 88)
³/₄ cup corn flour
¹/₄ cup cornmeal
1 tablespoon granulated sugar
2 teaspoons baking soda
1¹/₂ teaspoons salt
1 teaspoon xanthan gum
6 tablespoons canola or corn oil
¹/₄ cup Grade B maple syrup
1 tablespoon pureed pear baby food

Cornbread is the quintessential accompaniment to chili, and this recipe will not disappoint. None of my taste testers knew this was allergen-free, which to me, is the hallmark of a successful recipe.

Serves 9

Preheat the oven to 400°F. Lightly grease an 8 x 8-inch square baking pan with canola oil.

In a cup, make "buttermilk" by combining the rice milk and cider vinegar. In a large mixing bowl, whisk together the baking mix, corn flour, cornmeal, sugar, baking soda, salt, and xanthan gum.

In a medium bowl, add the "buttermilk" mixture, oil, maple syrup, and pureed pear baby food. Stir to combine the mixture, then pour it over the dry ingredients. Stir the batter until it is smooth and thoroughly combined.

Pour the batter into the prepared pan and bake for 20 minutes, or until the top is golden and a toothpick inserted in the center comes out clean.

Let cool for 20 minutes in the pan on a cooling rack. Cut it into squares and serve warm with jelly or honey or with something savory like chili.

This cornbread is best eaten the day it is baked.

apple-cinnamon streusel muffins

Streusel Topping
- 1 cup Betsy's Baking Mix (see page 88)
- ½ cup packed light brown sugar
- ¼ teaspoon ground cinnamon
- ¼ teaspoon salt
- ¼ teaspoon xanthan gum
- ½ cup organic palm fruit oil shortening

Muffins
- 1 cup gluten-free vanilla rice milk
- 1 teaspoon cider vinegar
- 3 tablespoons water
- 1 tablespoon ground flaxseed meal
- 2 cups Betsy's Baking Mix (see page 88)
- 2 tablespoons granulated sugar
- 1 tablespoon baking powder
- 1 teaspoon xanthan gum
- ½ teaspoon baking soda
- ½ teaspoon ground cinnamon
- ½ teaspoon salt
- ¼ cup liquefied organic refined coconut oil (stir before measuring if not completely liquid)
- ½ cup peeled and finely diced apples
- ⅓ cup raisins

Eat these delicious breakfast muffins warm and spread with apple butter for even greater autumnal flavor.

Serves 12

Preheat the oven to 375°F. Line 12 muffin tins with paper liners.

To make the streusel topping, combine the baking mix, brown sugar, cinnamon, salt, and xanthan gum in a medium bowl. Using a pastry blender or 2 knives, cut in the shortening until large clumps form, being careful not to overmix. Place the streusel in the freezer for at least 1 hour.

To make the muffins, in a small bowl, make "buttermilk" by combining the rice milk and cider vinegar. In another small bowl, combine the water and flaxseed meal and allow to thicken for 3 to 5 minutes. In a large mixing bowl, whisk together the baking mix, sugar, baking powder, xanthan gum, baking soda, cinnamon, and salt. With a spoon, create a well in the center of the dry ingredients.

In another bowl, thoroughly combine the "buttermilk" mixture, the thickened flaxseed mixture, and the coconut oil. Add the combined liquid ingredients all at once to the well in the dry ingredients and stir until combined. Fold in the apples and raisins.

Spoon the mixture into the prepared muffin tins. Sprinkle the muffins with the streusel topping. Bake the muffins for 18 to 20 minutes, or until golden brown on top and a toothpick inserted in the centers comes out clean. Cool in the tins on a cooling rack for 10 minutes, then eat warm or remove the muffins from the tins and cool completely on the cooling rack.

Store the completely cooled muffins in an airtight container and refrigerated for up to 3 days.

lickety-split **breads**

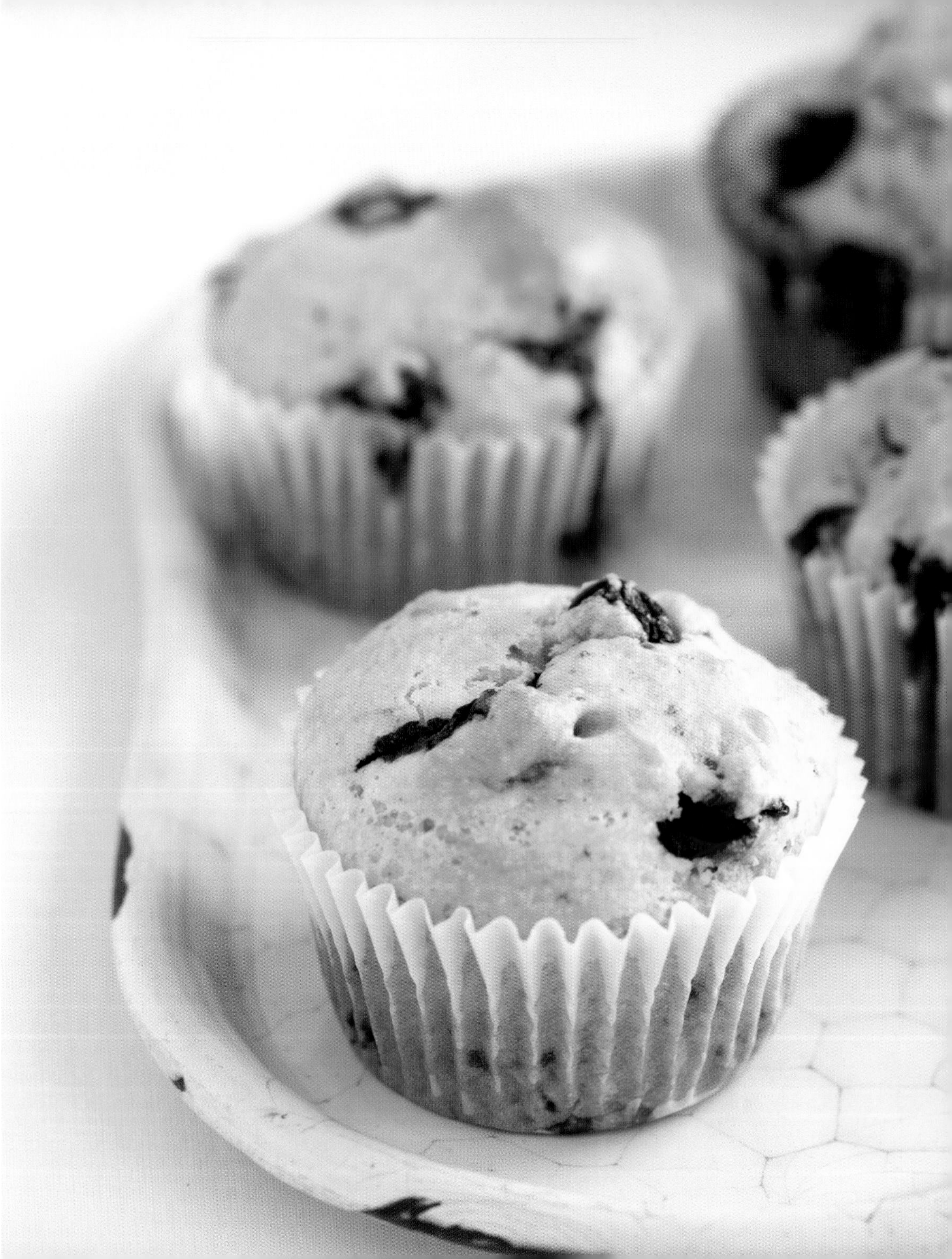

blueberry muffins

1 cup gluten-free vanilla rice milk
1 teaspoon cider vinegar
3 tablespoons water
1 tablespoon ground flaxseed meal
2 cups Betsy's Baking Mix (see page 88)
$\frac{1}{2}$ cup granulated sugar
1 tablespoon baking powder
1 teaspoon xanthan gum
$\frac{1}{2}$ teaspoon baking soda
$\frac{1}{2}$ teaspoon salt
$\frac{1}{4}$ cup liquefied organic refined coconut oil (stir before measuring if not completely liquid)
1 cup fresh blueberries

Muffins are such an all-American breakfast staple that I practiced this recipe over and over again until I got them right. I took the extras to friends, and after so many tastings, they now refer to me as "The Muffin Lady." These are a very homey, rustic, and old-fashioned homage to the blueberry muffin.

Serves 12

Preheat the oven to 375°F. Line 12 muffin cups with paper liners.

In a small bowl, make "buttermilk" by combining the rice milk and cider vinegar. In another small bowl, combine the water and flaxseed meal and allow to thicken for 3 to 5 minutes. In a large mixing bowl, whisk together the baking mix, sugar, baking powder, xanthan gum, baking soda, and salt until well combined. With a spoon, create a well in the center of the dry ingredients.

In another bowl, thoroughly combine the "buttermilk" mixture, the thickened flaxseed mixture, and the coconut oil. Add the combined liquid ingredients all at once to the well in the dry ingredients and stir until combined. Fold in the blueberries.

Spoon the batter into the prepared muffin tins. Bake for 18 to 20 minutes, or until golden brown on top and a toothpick inserted in the centers comes out clean. Let cool in the tins on a cooling rack for 10 minutes. Remove the muffins from the tins and cool them completely on the cooling rack.

Store the completely cooled muffins in an airtight container and refrigerated for up to 3 days.

" **Flaxseed is loaded with health**

benefits.

High in alpha lignans and omega-3s, it is good for your heart and skin. "

cranberry orange bread

6 tablespoons water
2 tablespoons ground
    flaxseed meal
2¼ cups Betsy's Baking Mix
    (see page 88)
1 cup granulated sugar
1 tablespoon baking powder
1 teaspoon xanthan gum
½ teaspoon baking soda
½ teaspoon salt
    Freshly grated zest of 1
    orange
½ cup gluten-free plain rice
    milk
½ cup orange juice
¼ cup canola oil
1½ cups fresh cranberries

The inspiration for this bread came to me from a very good, very Southern friend who was skeptical about eliminating the butter and eggs from anything. I worked on the recipe until I knew that I could make her proud.

Each loaf serves 8

Preheat the oven to 325°F. Grease two 9 x 5-inch loaf pans with canola oil.

In a small bowl, mix together the water and flaxseed meal and allow to thicken for 3 to 5 minutes. In a large mixing bowl, whisk together the baking mix, sugar, baking powder, xanthan gum, baking soda, salt, and orange zest. With a spoon, create a well in the center. In another bowl, stir together the rice milk, juice, and oil.

Pour the liquid mixture, as well as the flaxseed mixture, into the well in the dry ingredients, then stir until thoroughly combined; there will still be a few lumps. Fold in the cranberries.

Pour the batter into the prepared pans. Bake for 50 minutes, or until a toothpick inserted in the centers comes out clean. (If the loaves appear to be browning too fast, reduce the temperature to 300°F.) Cool completely in the pans on cooling racks.

Store the completely cooled breads, tightly wrapped and refrigerated, for up to 5 days, or freeze for up to 3 months.

zucchini bread

9 tablespoons water
3 tablespoons ground
   flaxseed meal
3 cups Betsy's Baking Mix
   (see page 88)
2 teaspoons baking soda
1½ teaspoons ground
   cinnamon
1 teaspoon salt
1 teaspoon xanthan gum
½ teaspoon baking powder
2 cups granulated sugar
1 cup canola oil
2 teaspoons vanilla extract
2 cups grated zucchini

In Ohio in the summer, no one can eat the zucchini from their gardens fast enough. Inevitably, a lot of the zucchini ends up in zucchini bread that goes into the freezer to be eaten year-round. I particularly like to eat it with a big Cobb salad or even as a dessert.

Serves 8

Preheat the oven to 350°F. Lightly grease a 9 x 5-inch loaf pan with canola oil.

In a small bowl, mix together the water and flaxseed meal and allow to thicken for 3 to 5 minutes. In a large bowl, whisk together the baking mix, baking soda, cinnamon, salt, xanthan gum, and baking powder.

In the bowl of a stand mixer, cream together the sugar and canola oil for 1 minute on medium speed. Beat in the flaxseed mixture, then scrape down the sides of the bowl. Beat in the vanilla, then pour in the dry ingredients and mix until thoroughly combined. Fold in the zucchini.

Pour the batter into the prepared pan. Bake for 1½ hours, or until the top is golden and a toothpick inserted in the center comes out clean. Cool for 45 minutes in the pan before removing the cake from the pan and placing on a cooling rack to cool completely.

Store the completely cooled bread, tightly wrapped and refrigerated, for up to 3 to 5 days, or freeze for up to 3 months.

free-form raspberry scones

½ cup gluten-free vanilla rice milk

½ teaspoon cider vinegar

3 tablespoons water

1 tablespoon ground flaxseed meal

2 cups Betsy's Baking Mix (see page 88)

⅓ cup granulated sugar

1 teaspoon baking powder

1 teaspoon baking soda

1 teaspoon xanthan gum

¼ teaspoon salt

6 tablespoons organic palm fruit oil shortening

¾ cup fresh raspberries

⅓ cup gluten-, soy-, dairy-, egg-, and nut-free semisweet chocolate chips, optional

2 teaspoons vanilla extract

One day I was making scones on a limited time table, and instead of rolling them out, I just spooned them onto baking sheets. They tasted just as good, and they were so much easier!

Serves 16

Preheat the oven to 375°F and line a baking sheet with parchment paper.

In a small bowl or cup, make "buttermilk" by combining the rice milk and cider vinegar. In another small bowl, combine the water and flaxseed meal and allow to thicken for 3 to 5 minutes.

In a large bowl, whisk together the baking mix, sugar, baking powder, baking soda, xanthan gum, and salt. With a pastry blender or 2 knives, cut in the shortening until the mixture resembles coarse crumbs. Stir in the raspberries and the chocolate chips, if you are using them.

In a small separate bowl, whisk together the "buttermilk" mixture, the flaxseed mixture, and the vanilla. Add the combined liquid ingredients to the dry ingredients and stir just until combined.

With a small ice cream scoop, scoop the scones about 2 inches apart onto the prepared baking sheet. Bake for about 18 minutes, or until the tops are golden. Allow the scones to cool on the baking sheets on cooling racks for 10 minutes, then transfer the scones directly onto the cooling racks to cool completely.

These scones are best eaten on the day they are made.

pumpkin bread

¾ cup water
½ cup ground flaxseed meal
3 cups Betsy's Baking Mix
   (see page 88)
2 teaspoons baking soda
1 teaspoon ground cinnamon
1 teaspoon ground cloves
1 teaspoon salt
1 teaspoon xanthan gum
½ teaspoon baking powder
2 cups granulated sugar
⅔ cup canola oil
   One 15-ounce can solid
      pack pureed pumpkin
½ cup raisins, optional

Pumpkin bread makes me think of fall and crisp Sunday afternoons spent jumping in giant piles of raked leaves.

Each loaf serves 8

Preheat the oven to 350°F. Lightly grease two 9 x 5-inch loaf pans with canola oil.

In a small bowl, combine the water and flaxseed meal and allow to thicken for 3 to 5 minutes. In a large bowl, whisk together the baking mix, baking soda, cinnamon, cloves, salt, xanthan gum, and baking powder.

In the bowl of a stand mixer, cream together the sugar and canola oil for 1 minute on medium speed. Add the pumpkin puree and beat for another minute. Scrape down the sides of the bowl, add the flaxseed mixture, and beat for another minute. Scrape down the sides again and add the dry ingredients. Mix the batter on low speed for 30 seconds. Scrape down the sides, then beat the batter for 45 seconds. Fold in the raisins, if you are using them.

Pour the batter into the prepared pans and bake for 1 hour, or until the tops are golden and a toothpick inserted in the centers comes out clean. Let the pumpkin breads cool completely in the pans on cooling racks before slicing.

Store the completely cooled breads, tightly wrapped and refrigerated, for up to 5 days, or freeze for up to 3 months.

blueberry crumb cake

Streusel Topping
- 1 cup Betsy's Baking Mix (see page 88)
- 1/2 cup packed light brown sugar
- 1/4 teaspoon ground cinnamon
- 1/4 teaspoon salt
- 1/4 teaspoon xanthan gum
- 1/2 cup organic palm fruit oil shortening, chilled

Cake
- 1/4 cup gluten-free vanilla rice milk
- 1/4 teaspoon cider vinegar
- 3 tablespoons water
- 1 tablespoon ground flaxseed meal
- 1 1/2 cups plus 1 teaspoon Betsy's Baking Mix (see page 88)
- 1 1/2 teaspoons baking powder
- 1/2 teaspoon baking soda
- 1/2 teaspoon salt
- 1/2 teaspoon xanthan gum
- 1/4 teaspoon ground allspice
- 3/4 cup granulated sugar
- 1/4 cup organic palm fruit oil shortening
- 1 1/2 cups fresh blueberries

I love to bring this cake to my daughter's school when we have classroom get-togethers. It pairs equally well with coffee and orange juice, and everybody always gobbles it up right down to the last crumb.

Serves 6 to 8

Preheat the oven to 350°F. Lightly grease a 9 x 5-inch loaf pan with canola oil.

To make the streusel topping, in a medium bowl, whisk together the baking mix, brown sugar, cinnamon, salt, and xanthan gum. With a pastry blender or 2 knives, cut in the shortening until large clumps form. Place the streusel in the freezer for at least 1 hour.

blueberry crumb cake

To make the cake, in a small bowl, make "buttermilk" by combining the rice milk and cider vinegar. In another small bowl, combine the water and flaxseed meal and allow to thicken for 3 to 5 minutes. In a large bowl, whisk together 1½ cups of the baking mix, the baking powder, baking soda, salt, xanthan gum, and allspice.

In the bowl of a stand mixer, cream together the sugar and shortening until light and fluffy. Add the flaxseed mixture and beat again, then scrape down the sides of the bowl. In alternating batches, add the "buttermilk" mixture and the dry ingredients, beginning and ending with the dry ingredients. In a small bowl, toss the blueberries with the remaining 1 teaspoon of baking mix, then fold them into the batter.

Spread the batter in the prepared loaf pan. Sprinkle it with the prepared streusel topping and bake for 1 hour and 15 minutes, or until the top is golden brown and a toothpick inserted in the center comes out clean. Remove the cake from the oven and let it cool in the pan on a cooling rack for 1 hour, then turn out the cake onto a cooling rack to cool completely.

Store the completely cooled cake, tightly wrapped and refrigerated, for up to 3 days.

cinnamon swirl rolls

Dough

- ½ cup warm gluten-free rice milk (105° to 110°F)
- ¼ cup granulated sugar
- 2 tablespoons warm water (105° to 110°F)
- 1½ teaspoons dry active yeast
- 3 tablespoons water
- 1 tablespoon ground flaxseed meal
- 3¾ cups Betsy's Baking Mix (see page 88)
- 1 teaspoon baking soda
- 1 teaspoon xanthan gum
- 1 teaspoon baking powder
- ½ teaspoon salt
- ¼ cup organic palm fruit oil shortening
- 2 tablespoons applesauce
- ½ cup raisins

Filling

- ¼ cup granulated sugar
- 2 teaspoons ground cinnamon
- 1 tablespoon organic palm fruit oil shortening

Hands down, this is my favorite recipe in this entire book. Inspired by both the French pain au raisin and the American Cinnabon, the texture is doughier. They are chewy and gooey and just like what we used to eat when I was growing up. I have burned my mouth more than once trying to eat these the minute they have come out of the oven.

Serves 12

Preheat the oven to 375°F.

To make the dough, mix together the warm rice milk, sugar, 2 tablespoons of warm water, and the yeast in a medium bowl. Allow the mixture to "proof" for 5 minutes. After 5 minutes, the top of the liquid should appear somewhat foamy. (If the yeast does not foam, then it is no longer good.)

While the yeast mixture is proofing, in a small bowl, mix together the 3 tablespoons of water and the flaxseed meal and allow to thicken for 3 to 5 minutes. In another small bowl, mix together the baking mix, baking soda, xanthan gum, baking powder, and salt. In the bowl of a stand mixer, cream together the shortening and applesauce. Stir in the flaxseed meal and mix in the dry ingredients until well combined. Stir in the yeast mixture. Fold in the raisins with a spatula. Cover the mixing bowl with a towel and place in a warm place to rise for 1 hour.

Meanwhile, to prepare the filling, combine the sugar and cinnamon in a small bowl. When the dough has risen, roll it out between 2 sheets of parchment paper to ½ inch thick; this should make a rectangle that is about 15 x 11 inches. Peel off the top sheet of parchment and spread the tablespoon of shortening over the dough. Sprinkle the dough with the cinnamon sugar, then, starting at the shorter end of the rectangle and using the parchment to help you roll the dough, tightly roll the dough into a long log. Smooth out any cracks in the dough with your fingers, from the outside of the parchment paper.

CONTINUED ON PAGE 80

lickety-split quick **breads**

CONTINUED FROM PAGE 78

cinnamon swirl rolls

Glaze
- ³⁄₄ **cup packed dark brown sugar**
- ¹⁄₄ **cup organic palm fruit oil shortening**
- 2 **tablespoons water**
- ¹⁄₄ **cup Lyle's Golden Syrup**

Using a very sharp knife, cut the log into 12 slices.

To make the glaze, heat the brown sugar, shortening, and water in a small saucepan over medium heat, stirring, until the shortening has melted. Stir in the Lyle's Golden Syrup, then spread the mixture on the bottom of a 9-inch round cake pan. Place the rolls, cut side down, on top of the glaze.

Bake the rolls for 20 minutes, or until they are golden brown. Immediately turn the rolls out onto a cooling rack placed on a sheet of parchment paper; the glaze will run down the sides of the rolls and drip onto the parchment. Serve the rolls warm or let them cool completely and spread them with my Vanilla Buttercream Frosting (see page 93), if desired.

Store these rolls in an airtight container and refrigerated for up to 2 days.

helpful tip: If you don't have a candy thermometer or an instant-read thermometer, here is an easy trick to tell if your rice milk and water are the right temperature: If you place a drop of the warm rice milk and warm water on the top of your lip, it should feel very warm but not hot enough to burn.

Bear in mind that this dough will rise much differently than a dough made of wheat flour. Do not be alarmed if the dough does not double or triple in size, it will still work.

how to grease a pan
with canola oil:

Pour a tablespoon or two of canola oil into a small ramekin or teacup. Dip a pastry brush or a clean (brand new) paintbrush into the oil and brush a thin layer of the oil across the bottom and sides of the baking pan. Make sure to cover the entire pan, paying extra attention that the oil has covered the places where the sides and the bottom of the pan meet.

   Alternatively, you may fill a spray bottle with canola oil and mist the inside of the pan.

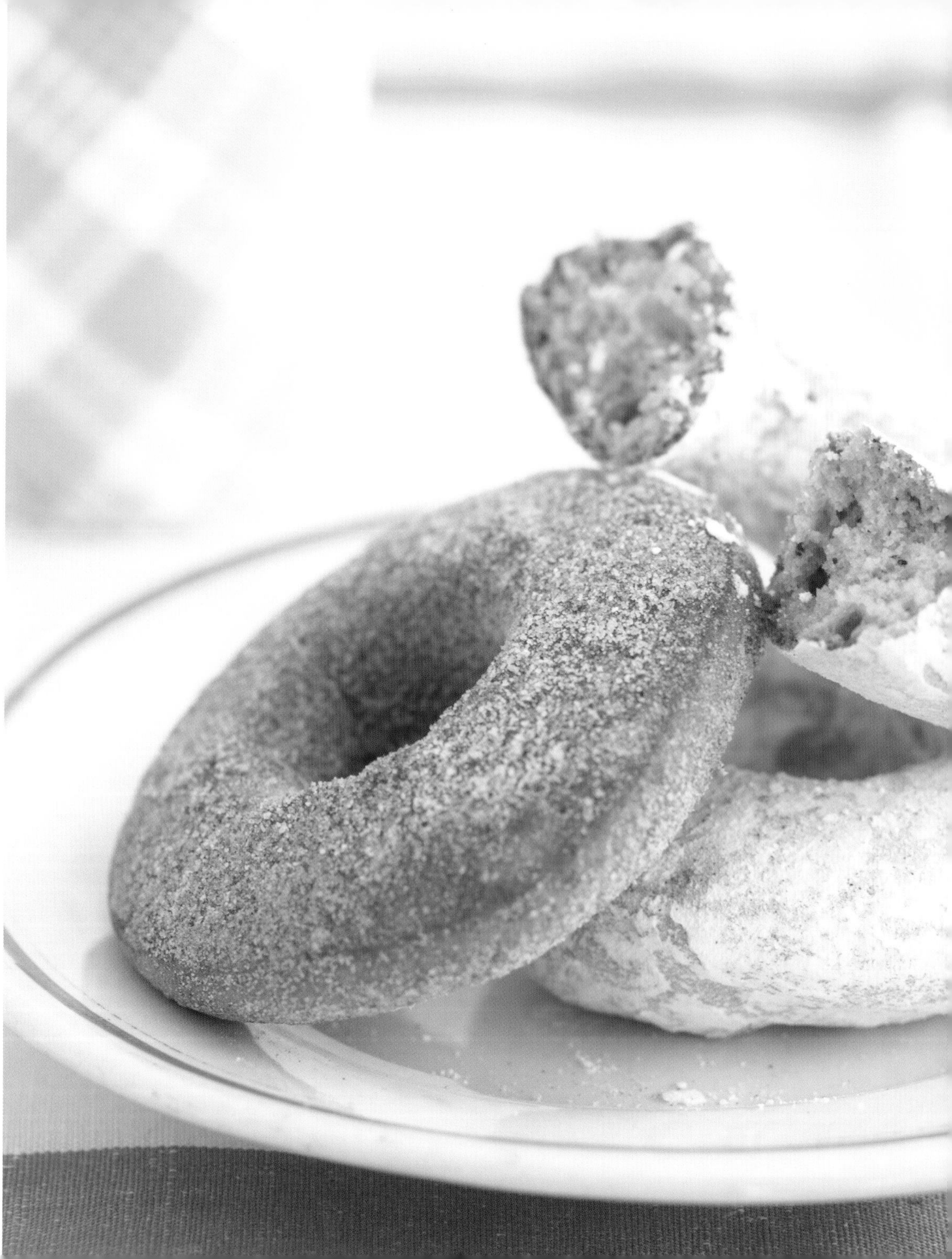

delicious baked donuts

½ cup gluten-free vanilla rice
  milk
½ teaspoon cider vinegar
3 tablespoons water
1 tablespoon ground
  flaxseed meal
1 cup granulated sugar
2 teaspoons baking powder
½ teaspoon baking soda
½ teaspoon salt
½ teaspoon xanthan gum
¼ teaspoon ground nutmeg
1¾ cups Betsy's Baking Mix
  (see page 88)
1 tablespoon organic
  refined coconut oil
  (stir before measuring if
  not completely liquid)
2 cups confectioners' sugar
2 teaspoons ground
  cinnamon
2 paper bags for coating the
  donuts

Donuts are a weekend treat for my husband and children. Without fail, my husband takes the girls for a powdered donut at our favorite gourmet food store, The Salamander, in Greenport, New York. I felt left out of the ritual, so I came up with these to satisfy my own love of fresh, warm donuts.

Serves 8

Preheat the oven to 350°F. Lightly grease 8 donut molds with canola oil.

In a small bowl, make "buttermilk" by combining the rice milk and cider vinegar. In another small bowl, mix together the water and flaxseed meal and allow to thicken for 3 to 5 minutes.

In a large mixing bowl, whisk together ½ cup of the granulated sugar, the baking powder, baking soda, salt, xanthan gum, and nutmeg. Stir in the flaxseed mixture and the "buttermilk" mixture. Gradually add the baking mix and stir until the dry ingredients are thoroughly combined but the dough is still soft. Spoon the dough into a large pastry bag fitted with a wide tip and pipe the batter into the prepared molds.

CONTINUED ON PAGE 84

delicious baked doughnuts

Place the molds on a baking sheet and bake for about 18 minutes, or until the donuts are golden and firm. Remove the donuts from the oven and turn them out onto cooling racks to cool.

Pour the confectioners' sugar into 1 paper bag, and combine the cinnamon and the remaining ½ cup of granulated sugar the other bag. Drop the donuts into one bag or another and, holding the top of the bag tightly closed, shake the bag to thoroughly coat each donut. Serve immediately.

variation:
fried donuts

Heat a couple of inches of canola oil in a deep pot to 360°F.
Prepare the donuts as instructed, but instead of spooning the batter into a pastry bag, carefully drop it by large spoonfuls into the hot canola oil, without crowding, and fry for 1 to 2 minutes per side, or until golden. Remove the donuts from the oil with a slotted spoon an d drain them on paper towels. Continue with the remaining dough. Then continue with coating the donuts as instructed above. Serve immediately.

silver dollar pancakes

½ cup gluten-free vanilla rice milk

½ teaspoon cider vinegar

1 tablespoon plus 1½ teaspoons water

1½ teaspoons ground flaxseed meal

½ cup Betsy's Baking Mix (see page 88)

1 tablespoon granulated sugar

1 teaspoon baking powder

¼ teaspoon baking soda

¼ teaspoon salt

⅛ teaspoon xanthan gum

½ cup gluten-, soy-, dairy-, egg-, and nut-free semisweet chocolate chips, raisins, diced apples, blueberries, or diced bananas, optional

Confectioners' sugar or Grade B maple syrup for serving

Pancakes are my daughters' favorite way to start their day. Smothered in maple syrup, but free of eggs, wheat, soy, milk, and nuts, these pancakes taste just like what I remember eating as a child. My girls like to add chocolate chips, raisins, diced apples, or diced bananas to the batter before cooking as a special treat.

Makes 20 pancakes, about 4 servings

Lightly grease a griddle or large frying pan with canola oil and heat over medium heat.

Meanwhile, in a small bowl, make "buttermilk" by combining the rice milk and cider vinegar. In another small bowl, combine the water and flaxseed meal and allow to thicken for 3 to 5 minutes.

In a large bowl, thoroughly combine the baking mix, sugar, baking powder, baking soda, salt, and xanthan gum. Add the flaxseed mixture and the "buttermilk" mixture to the dry ingredients and stir just until thoroughly moistened. If using, fold in the chocolate chips or fruit.

Spoon the batter onto the preheated griddle by heaping tablespoonfuls. While cooking, the pancakes will begin to bubble. Cook for 3 to 4 minutes, or until most of the bubbles have burst. Then flip the pancakes and cook until the other side is golden brown. Serve with confectioner's sugar or syrup.

These pancakes are best eaten right away but can be stored with pieces of wax paper between the cakes in an airtight container and frozen for up to 3 months. To reheat, place the pancakes in a single layer on parchment-lined baking sheets and bake at 200°F for 10 minutes, or until heated through.

you can have your

cake

and eat it too

Although cookies are the main staple of Betsy & Claude Baking Co., cake is really my favorite dessert. Moist and tender and piled high with fluffy buttercream, I cannot think of anything more divine. I also love to decorate them. When I found out that I was allergic to wheat and eggs, I could no sooner imagine a cup of coffee let alone my next birthday without a thick slice of yellow cake with chocolate frosting sandwiched between the layers and swirled on top. Fortunately, I came up with the next best thing.

Now no one has to pass on a cupcake or wonder how birthday cake tastes. The centerpiece of so many celebrations like weddings, birthdays, going away parties, and baby showers, cake is an important part of the American culture, and now everyone can partake and enjoy.

betsy's baking mix

3¾ cups garbanzo bean flour
2¼ cups potato starch
1½ cups tapioca flour

As I was working on this book, I found that most of my cake and quick bread recipes used the same ratio of flours. So I thought it would just be easier to make one master mix to have on hand any time you are in the mood to bake, rather than having to measure several flours each time. Make this in large batches and then store it in an airtight container in a cool place for up to 3 months. It will make your baking experience much faster, easier, and neater. I keep my mix in the freezer to ensure its freshness. Just make sure to thoroughly whisk it every single time before using it.

Makes enough for about 3 cakes

Measure all of the flours into a large container that has an airtight lid.

Stir very well with a wire whisk until evenly incorporated and no white spots remain. Then seal the container and shake it vigorously for 1 minute.

Store the baking mix in a cool, dry place for up to 3 months, making sure to whisk it each time before measuring it.

helpful tip: It is so important to whisk this blend very well every time before using. Otherwise, you may not get the appropriate ratio of flours in your recipe.

claude's cake mix

4½ cups Betsy's Baking Mix
    (see page 88)
¾ cup cornstarch

This is my allergen-free version of "cake flour." The addition of the cornstarch simply makes my regular flour blend lighter and therefore better suited to some cake recipes. Make sure to store this in an airtight container in a cool, dry place and whisk it very well before using it.

Makes enough for about 2 cakes

Pour the baking mix into a large container that has an airtight lid. Whisk in the cornstarch until well combined and no white spots remain.

    Store the mixture in the airtight container for up to 3 months, making sure to whisk it before each use.

coconut cake

2½ cups Betsy's Baking Mix
    (see page 88)
1 teaspoon baking powder
1 teaspoon xanthan gum
½ teaspoon baking soda
½ teaspoon salt
9 tablespoons water
3 tablespoons ground
    flaxseed meal
1 cup well-shaken,
    unsweetened coconut
    milk (not light)
1 teaspoon cider vinegar
1 cup canola oil
1 cup granulated sugar
2 teaspoons vanilla extract
    One 7-ounce bag
    sweetened flaked coconut,
    plus another 7-ounce bag
    for decorating cake,
    optional
1 recipe Vanilla Buttercream
    Frosting (recipe follows)

One of our very good friends loves this cake and insists that I make it for her birthday every year. It is especially delicious slathered with lots of Vanilla Buttercream Frosting.

Serves 8 to 10

Position a rack in the center of the oven and preheat the oven to 350°F. Lightly grease three 8-inch round cake pans with canola oil, line the bottoms of the pans with parchment paper, and then lightly grease the parchment paper with a little more canola oil.

In a small bowl, whisk together the baking mix, baking powder, xanthan gum, baking soda, and salt. In another small bowl, combine the water and flaxseed meal and allow to thicken for 3 to 5 minutes. In a separate bowl, make "buttermilk" by combining the coconut milk and cider vinegar.

In the bowl of a stand mixer, cream together the canola oil and sugar on medium speed until thoroughly combined. With the mixer on low, blend in the flaxseed mixture. Scrape down the sides of the bowl, add the vanilla, and then beat the batter for 1 minute.

Scrape down the sides of the bowl again and then, with the mixer on low, alternately add the dry ingredients and the "buttermilk" mixture to the batter, ending with the dry ingredients. Mix the batter until the flour is thoroughly combined. Fold in the flaked coconut from one 7-ounce bag.

CONTINUED FROM PAGE 90

coconut cake

Pour the batter into the prepared pans, smoothing with a knife or spatula. Bake in the center of the oven for 40 minutes, or until the tops are golden brown and a toothpick inserted in the centers comes out clean.

Let the cakes cool completely in the pans on a cooling rack. Turn the cakes out of the pans and remove the parchment paper. Frost the top of each layer with the frosting. Transfer 1 layer to a serving plate and stack the other layers on top. Frost the sides of the cake. If desired, for a decorative effect, sprinkle the flaked coconut from the second bag over the top of the cake and gently press the coconut onto the sides.

Store the cake, covered and refrigerated, for up to 3 days.

"**Always cream the shortening and the** sugar **until light and fluffy before proceeding to the next step.** "

vanilla buttercream frosting

2 cups organic palm fruit oil shortening
2 cups Marshmallow Cream (see page 129)
3 cups confectioners' sugar, sifted
1 tablespoon vanilla extract
½ teaspoon salt

Of every recipe that I have ever developed, vanilla frosting has absolutely been the biggest challenge of all. However, I am very pleased with the outcome of this one. It is very versatile and works for everything from a cake frosting to the filling for whoopie pies to a decadent topping for cinnamon rolls.

Makes enough to generously frost and fill one 8-inch layer cake or 24 cupcakes

In the bowl of a stand mixer, beat together the shortening and the marshmallow cream on medium-high speed for 3 minutes. Scrape down the sides of the bowl, add the confectioners' sugar, and beat until the mixture is light and fluffy.

Blend in the vanilla and salt until thoroughly combined.

The frosting may be used immediately or stored in an airtight container and refrigerated for up to 1 week.

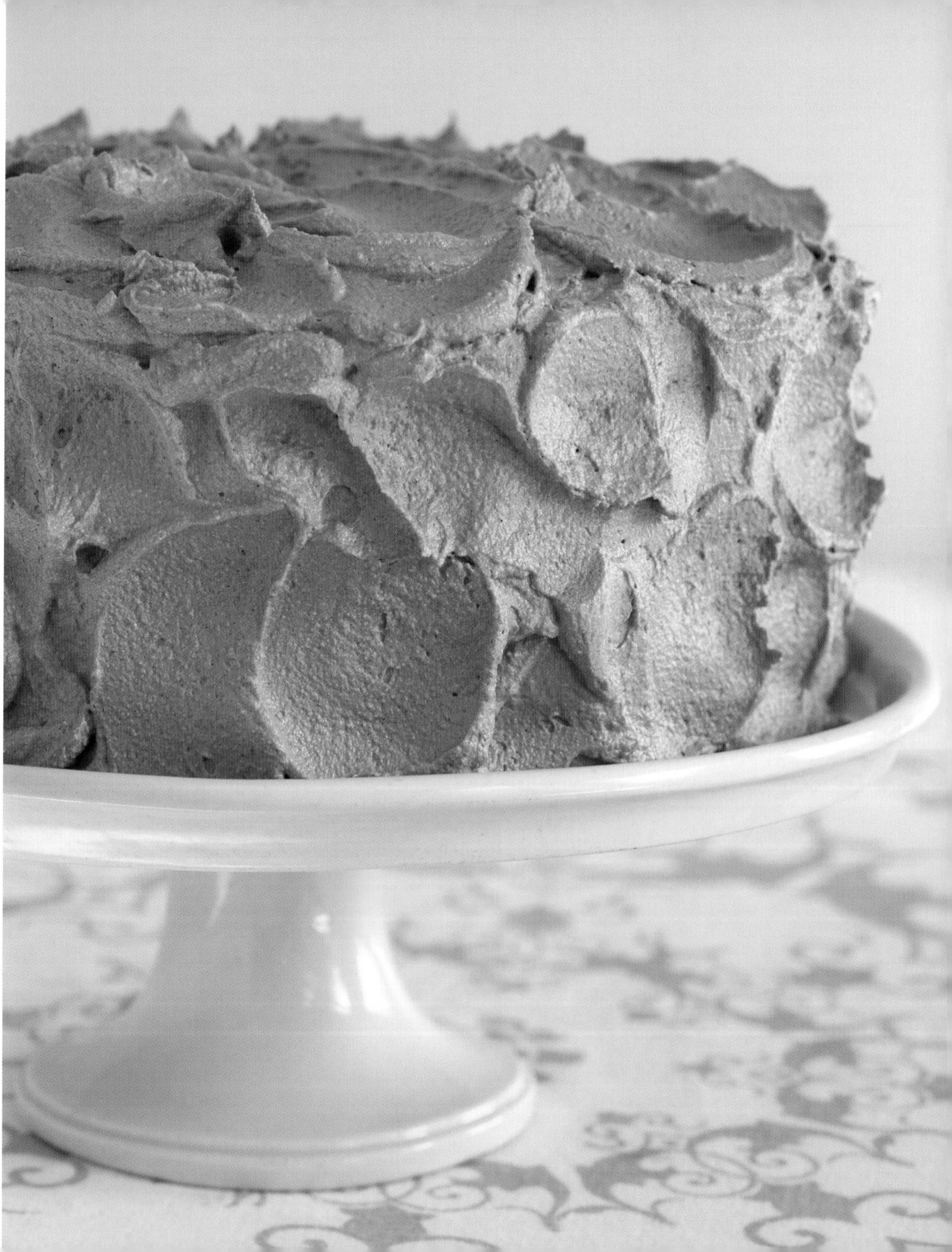

moist vanilla cake

6 tablespoons water
2 tablespoons ground
   flaxseed meal
1 cup well-shaken
   unsweetened coconut
   milk (not light)
1 teaspoon cider vinegar
3½ cups Betsy's Baking Mix
   (see page 88)
1 tablespoon plus 1 teaspoon
   baking powder
1 teaspoon baking soda
1 teaspoon xanthan gum
2 cups granulated sugar
½ cup organic palm fruit oil
   shortening
2 teaspoons vanilla extract
1 recipe Chocolate
   Buttercream Frosting
   (recipe follows)

In my opinion, the perfect birthday cake is a moist, delicious vanilla cake covered with piles of fluffy buttercream frosting and candles. This is the quintessential birthday cake for those of us with food allergies, and it is especially yummy with the Chocolate Buttercream Frosting.

Serves 8 to 10

Position a rack in the center of the oven and preheat the oven to 350°F. Lightly grease three 8-inch round cake pans with canola oil and line with parchment paper.

In a small bowl, combine the water and flaxseed meal and allow to thicken for 3 to 5 minutes. In another small bowl, make "buttermilk" by combining the coconut milk and cider vinegar.

In a large mixing bowl, mix together the baking mix, baking powder, baking soda, and xanthan gum. In the bowl of a stand mixer, beat the sugar and shortening until they are light and fluffy. Then blend in the flaxseed mixture and the vanilla. Alternately stir in the dry ingredients and the "buttermilk" mixture, starting and ending with the dry ingredients.

Pour the batter into the prepared pans and smooth it out with a knife or spatula. Bake the cakes for 25 minutes, or until the tops are golden and a toothpick inserted in the centers comes out clean.

Let the cakes cool completely in the pans on a cooling rack. Turn the cake layers out and frost the tops of each layer with the frosting. Transfer 1 layer to a serving plate and stack the other layers on top. Frost the sides of the cake.

Store the frosted cake, covered and refrigerated, for up to 3 days.

chocolate buttercream frosting

3 ounces unsweetened
   chocolate, chopped
1 recipe Vanilla Buttercream
   Frosting (see page 93)

Makes enough to fill and frost one 8-inch layer cake or 24 cupcakes

In the top of a double boiler set over simmering water, melt the chocolate, stirring occasionally, until it is smooth. Remove from the heat and set aside for 5 minutes.

Place the frosting in the bowl of a stand mixer and pour in the cooled melted chocolate. Beat the chocolate and frosting together until the frosting is fluffy and the chocolate is evenly mixed in. This frosting is best used on the day it is made.

very vanilla vegan buttercream frosting

1 cup organic refined coconut oil (stir before measuring if not completely liquid)
2 tablespoons cornstarch
2 14-ounce chilled cans unsweetened coconut milk
3/4 cup agave syrup
1 1/4 teaspoons vanilla extract
Pinch of salt
24 cooled cupcakes of your choice

Since most of my recipes are vegan, with the exception of my Vanilla Buttercream Frosting (see page 93), Marshmallow Cream (see page 129), and Lemon Squares (see page 54), I thought it only fair to include a suitable vegan frosting alternative. This creamy and delicious frosting must be refrigerated right up until moments before serving since it is made with coconut oil and will melt above 75°F. Because of this frosting's low melting point and consistency, I prefer to use it only on cupcakes. This way it doesn't have time to melt before the cakes are frosted and popped in the refrigerator.

Makes enough to frost 24 cupcakes

note: This frosting is not an appropriate substitute for the Top Hats recipe (see page 113), as it will melt if dipped into warm chocolate.

note: Working with this frosting is not like working with regular buttercream. To use: while the frosting is still creamy but has chilled and thickened considerably, mound a heaping spoonful of the frosting onto the top of each cupcake, swirl with a knife, and then refrigerate the cupcake until the frosting has hardened to a chilled buttercream consistency.

In a small saucepan, whisk together the coconut oil and cornstarch until the cornstarch is completely dissolved. Bring to a simmer over low heat and cook for 1 minute, whisking constantly. Remove from the heat and set aside to cool to room temperature.

Skim 1 cup of the coconut "cream" from the top of the chilled coconut milk in the cans (do not shake the cans in order to keep the milk and cream separate.) Combine the coconut "cream," agave syrup, vanilla, and salt in the pitcher of a high-speed blender. With the blender running, pour in the cooled oil mixture in a steady stream, in order to emulsify the mixture. Blend on high speed for 2 minutes. Pour the mixture into a metal bowl and refrigerate for at least 4 hours, stirring the frosting every hour or two.

When the frosting is completely chilled and has thickened to spreading consistency, remove it from the refrigerator and, working quickly, frost completely cooled cupcakes.

Store this frosting in the refrigerator and keep any items frosted with it in the refrigerator until just before serving. This frosting is best used the day it is made.

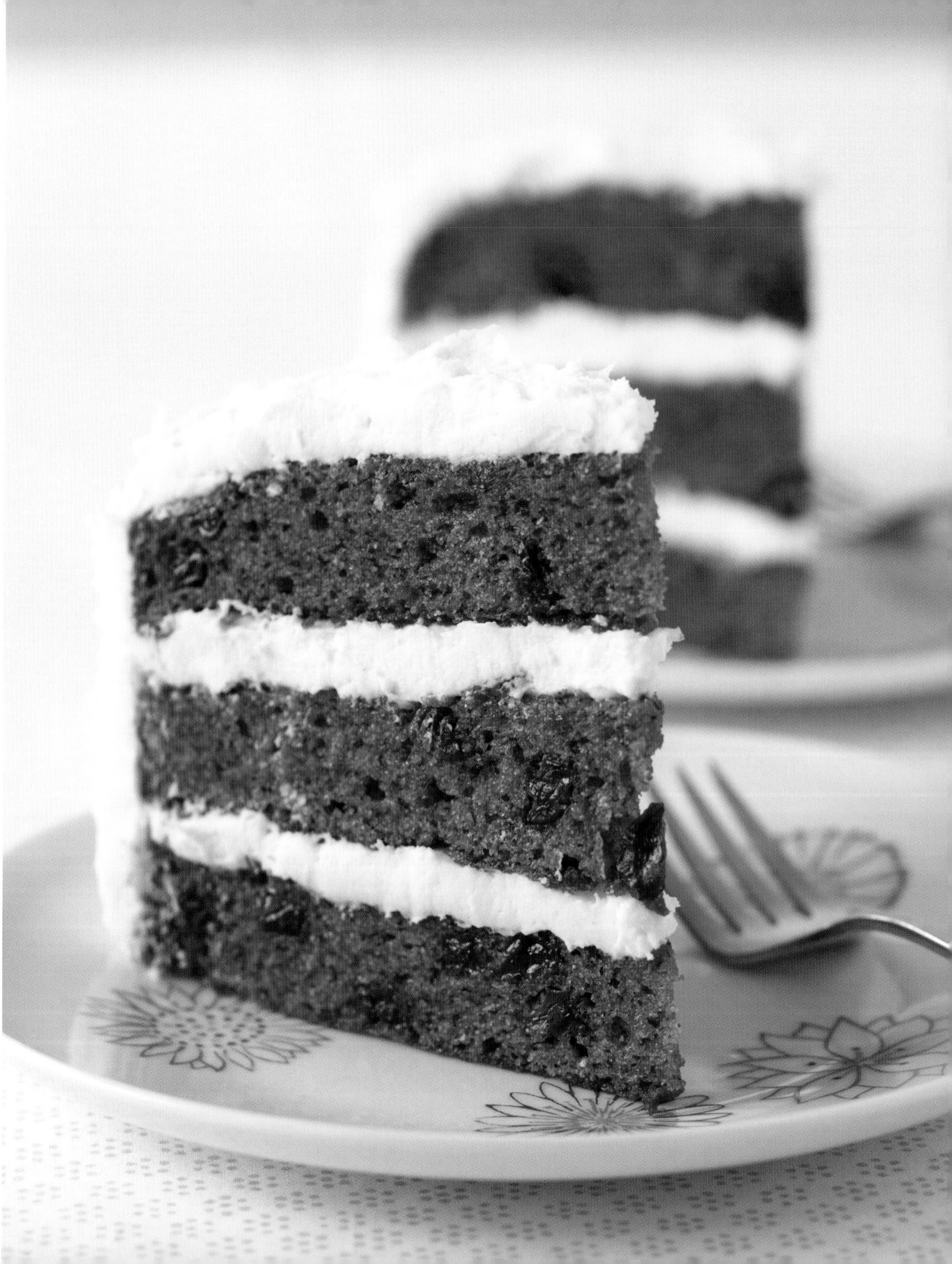

moist carrot cake

2 cups Betsy's Baking Mix (see page 88)
2 tablespoons ground ginger
2 teaspoons baking soda
2 teaspoons ground cinnamon
1 teaspoon xanthan gum
½ teaspoon salt
¾ cup water
¼ cup ground flaxseed meal
1½ cups granulated sugar
1⅓ cups canola oil
2 teaspoons vanilla extract
2 cups peeled grated carrots (about 4 large carrots)
1½ cups raisins
1 recipe Vanilla Buttercream Frosting (see page 93)

When I made this for the first time, I served it without telling anyone that it was gluten-, dairy-, soy-, nut-, and egg-free. One friend still swears it was the best carrot cake she's ever had, allergens or not.

Serves 8 to 10

Preheat the oven to 350°F. Lightly grease three 8-inch round cake pans with canola oil, line the bottoms of the pans with parchment paper, and then lightly grease the parchment paper.

In a large bowl, whisk together the baking mix, ginger, baking soda, cinnamon, xanthan gum, and salt. In a small bowl, combine the water and flaxseed meal and allow to thicken for 3 to 5 minutes.

In the bowl of a stand mixer, cream together the sugar and oil. Add in the vanilla and then the flaxseed mixture and beat for 1 minute. Stir in the dry ingredients and then fold in the shredded carrots and the raisins.

Pour the batter into the prepared pans, smooth the tops with a knife, and bake for 30 minutes, or until the cakes are golden and a toothpick inserted in the centers comes out clean.

Let the cakes cool completely in their pans on a cooling rack. Turn the cakes out of the pans and remove the parchment paper. Frost the top of each cake layer with the frosting. Transfer 1 layer to a serving plate and stack the other layers on top. Frost the sides of the cake.

Store the frosted cake, covered and refrigerated, for up to 3 days.

you can have your cake and eat it too

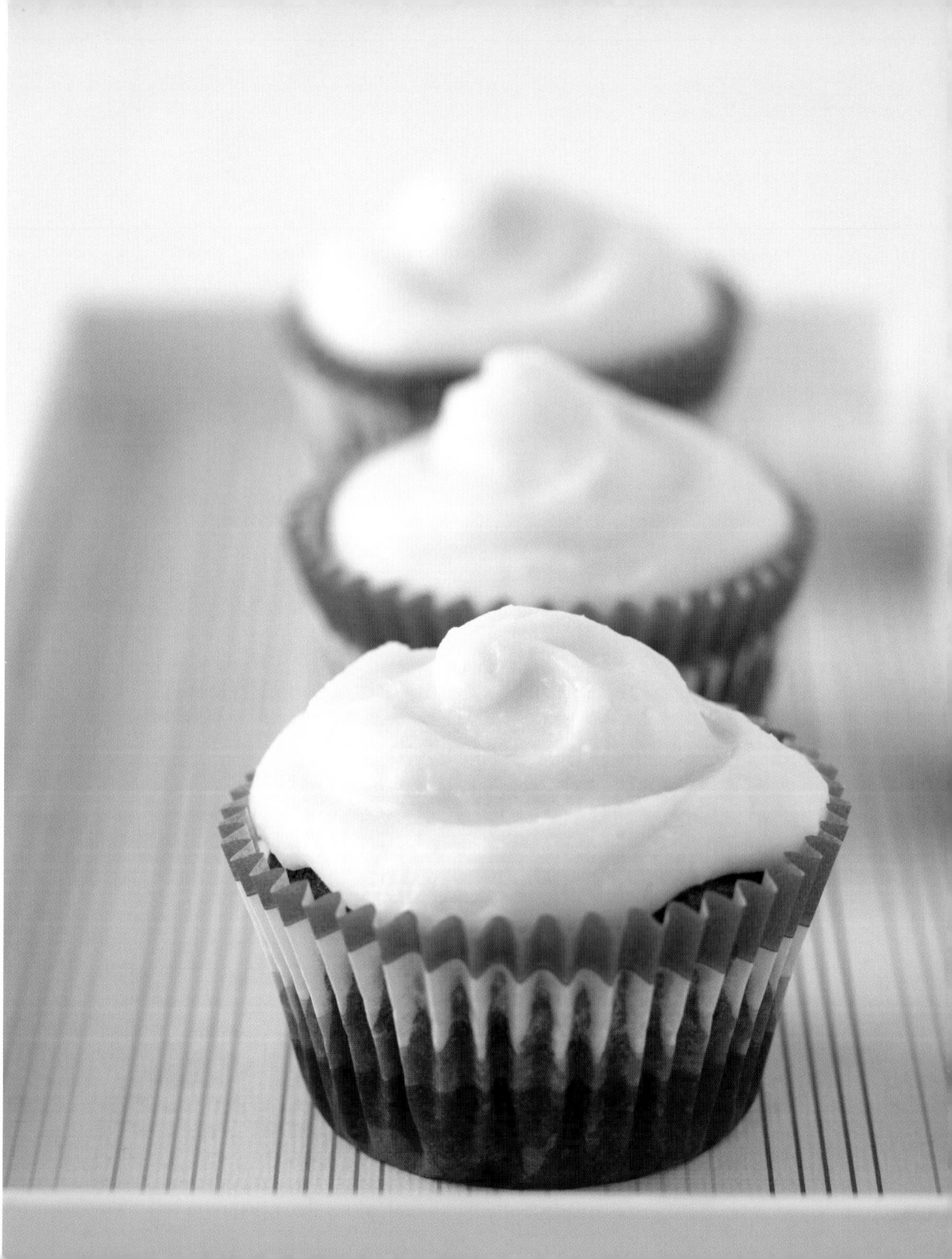

chocolate zucchini cupcakes

½ cup gluten-free vanilla rice milk

½ teaspoon cider vinegar

2½ cups Betsy's Baking Mix (see page 88)

¼ cup unsweetened cocoa powder

2 teaspoons baking soda

1 teaspoon xanthan gum

½ teaspoon ground allspice

½ teaspoon ground cinnamon

½ teaspoon salt

½ cup canola oil

½ cup organic palm fruit oil shortening

1 cup packed dark brown sugar

½ cup granulated sugar

1 teaspoon vanilla extract

2 cups unpeeled grated zucchini (about 2 medium zucchini)

1 recipe Very Vanilla Vegan Buttercream Frosting (see page 97)

Although this sounds like a strange combination, it is an allergen-reduced variation of something my aunt used to make every summer when zucchini were abundant in the Midwest. It is one of my favorites. No one will ever suspect that zucchini is what makes it so moist. While my aunt always frosted them with a cream cheese icing, they are great with either my Very Vanilla Vegan Buttercream Frosting (see page 93) or my original Vanilla Buttercream.

Makes 24 cupcakes

Preheat the oven to 350°F. Line 24 cupcake tins with paper liners.

In a small bowl, make "buttermilk" by combining the rice milk and cider vinegar. In a large bowl, whisk together the baking mix, cocoa powder, baking soda, xanthan gum, allspice, cinnamon, and salt.

In the bowl of a stand mixer, cream together the oil, shortening, and sugars until they are light and fluffy. Add the vanilla and beat for 1 minute. In 3 additions, alternately add the dry mixture and "buttermilk" mixture, beginning and ending with the dry ingredients and stirring well after each addition. Fold in the grated zucchini.

Scoop the batter into the lined cupcake tins and bake for 25 to 30 minutes, or until a toothpick inserted in the centers comes out clean. Let the cupcakes cool completely in their tins on a cooling rack. Remove the cupcakes from the tins.

Working quickly, mound a heaping spoonful of the chilled frosting onto the top of each cupcake, swirl the frosting with a knife, and then refrigerate the cupcakes until the frosting has hardened to a chilled buttercream consistency.

Store the frosted cupcakes, covered and refrigerated, for up to 3 days.

german chocolate cake

4   ounces gluten-, soy-, dairy-,
    egg-, and nut-free
    semisweet chocolate,
    chopped
1   cup gluten-free vanilla rice
    milk, divided
1   teaspoon cider vinegar
6   tablespoons water
2   tablespoons ground
    flaxseed meal
2⅓ cups Claude's Cake Mix
    (page 89)
1   teaspoon baking soda
1   teaspoon xanthan gum
½ teaspoon baking powder
½ teaspoon salt
1½ cups granulated sugar
⅔ cup organic palm fruit oil
    shortening
1   teaspoon vanilla extract
1   recipe German Chocolate
    Cake Frosting (recipe
    follows)

This was a birthday staple on my mother's side of the family. Sadly, the original recipe was never written down, so it has been lost, but I loved playing around with this recipe because the flavor conjures up so many fond memories. Don't feel limited by the German Chocolate Cake Frosting that follows. This is equally as delicious with my vanilla buttercream or chocolate buttercream, too.

Serves 8 to 10

Preheat the oven to 350°F. Grease two 9-inch round cake pans with canola oil, line the bottoms of the pans with parchment paper, and then lightly grease the parchment paper.

In the top of a double boiler set over simmering water, melt the chocolate, stirring until it is smooth. Remove it from the heat and set aside to cool.

In a small bowl, make "buttermilk" by combining the rice milk and cider vinegar. In another small bowl, combine the water and flaxseed meal and allow to thicken for 3 to 5 minutes. In a large mixing bowl, sift together the cake mix, baking soda, xanthan gum, baking powder, salt, and sugar.

In the bowl of a stand mixer, cream the shortening until it is light and fluffy. Scrape down the sides of the bowl and add the dry ingredient mixture, ¾ cup of the "buttermilk" mixture, and the vanilla. Mix the batter until it is moistened. Scrape down the sides of the bowl.

Stir in the melted, cooled chocolate, the flaxseed mixture, and the remaining ¼ cup of the "buttermilk" mixture. Beat the batter for 2 minutes, stopping to scrape down the bowl occasionally.

Pour the batter into the prepared pans and bake the cakes for 35 to 40 minutes, or until a toothpick inserted in the centers comes out clean.

german chocolate cake

Let the cakes cool completely in their pans on a cooling rack. Turn the cakes out of their pans and remove the parchment paper. Frost the top of each cake layer with the frosting. Transfer 1 layer to a serving plate, and then set the other layer on top. Frost the sides of the cake.

Store the frosted cake, covered and refrigerated, for up to 3 days.

german chocolate cake frosting

1 recipe Caramel
   Buttercream Frosting
   (see page 127)
2 ounces sweetened flaked
   coconut

Makes enough to fill and frost one 8-inch layer cake or 24 cupcakes

Beat the buttercream and coconut in the bowl of a stand mixer for 2 minutes, or until light, fluffy, and well combined. This frosting should be used immediately.

you can have your cake and eat it too

103

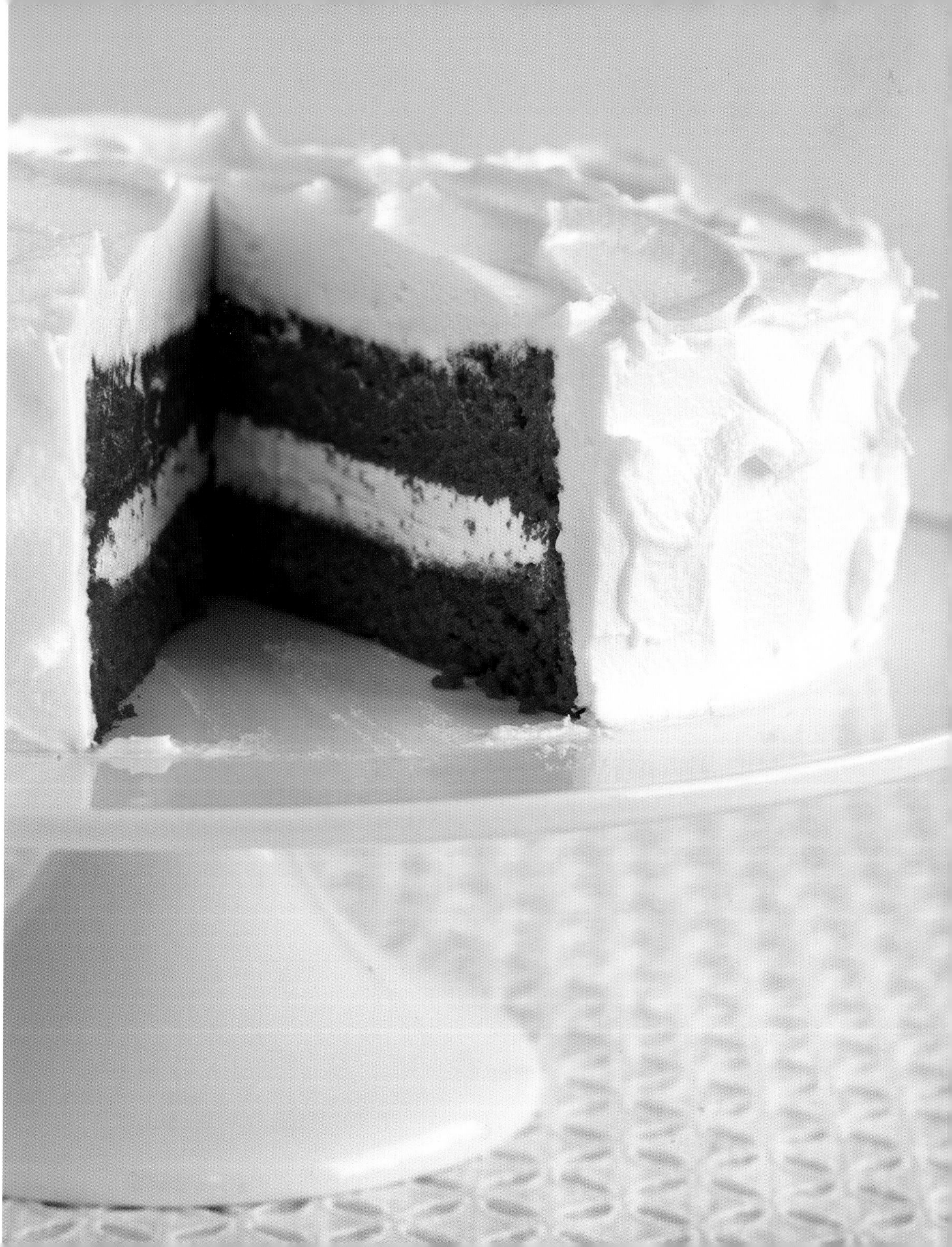

red velvet cake

1 cup gluten-free vanilla rice milk

1 teaspoon cider vinegar

2½ cups Betsy's Baking Mix (see page 88)

1 teaspoon salt

1 teaspoon xanthan gum

1½ cups granulated sugar

½ cup organic palm fruit oil shortening

2 tablespoons unsweetened cocoa powder

1 ounce red food coloring

¼ cup plus 3 tablespoons unsweetened applesauce

1 teaspoon vanilla extract

1 tablespoon gluten-free distilled white vinegar

1 teaspoon baking soda

1 recipe Vanilla Buttercream Frosting (see page 93)

I still remember the first time I ever heard of red velvet cake. Of course, it was in the movie *Steel Magnolias*, in the form of that infamously repulsive armadillo cake. However, the first time I tasted it was a totally different story. I loved it and wondered why its popularity hadn't spread above the Mason-Dixon Line. Now it has, so I felt this book wouldn't be complete without an allergen-free version of it.

Serves 8 to 10

Preheat the oven to 350°F. Grease two 9-inch round cake pans with canola oil, line the bottoms of the pans with parchment paper, and then lightly grease the parchment paper.

In a small bowl, make "buttermilk" by combining the rice milk and cider vinegar. In a large mixing bowl, combine the baking mix, salt, and xanthan gum.

In the bowl of a stand mixer, cream together the sugar and shortening. Meanwhile, in a separate small bowl, mix the cocoa powder and red food coloring to form a paste; set the paste aside. Add the applesauce and vanilla to the creamed shortening and sugar and blend until the mixture is light and creamy. Add the cocoa paste and mix well.

Alternately add the dry ingredients and the "buttermilk" mixture to the batter, beginning and ending with the dry ingredients.

Pour the white vinegar into a small cup and sprinkle the

CONTINUED ON PAGE 106

red velvet cake

baking soda over it. Immediately pour the fizzing combination into the cake batter and thoroughly combine the two mixtures.

Divide the batter between the prepared pans and bake the cakes for 30 to 35 minutes, or until a toothpick inserted in the centers comes out clean.

Let the cakes cool completely in their pans on a cooling rack. Turn the cakes out of their pans and remove the parchment paper. Frost the top of each cake layer with the frosting. Transfer 1 layer to a serving plate, and then set the other layer on top. Frost the sides of the cake.

Store the frosted cake, covered and refrigerated, for up to 3 days.

keeping layer cakes from
sticking to pans:

My mother uses this trick without fail. I always thought it was silly until I had my first cake stick to the bottom of a well-greased pan on the eve of an important event. From then on, I have used this one, too.

Lay one sheet of parchment paper on a work surface and place one of your round cake pans on top, right side up. Place your palm in the center of the pan in order to secure it in place. Then with a paring knife, run the blade around the edge of the pan. Remove the pan from the parchment and carefully punch out the circle along the perforation. Lightly brush the cake pan with canola oil, place the parchment round in the bottom of the pan, then brush the parchment with a very small amount of canola oil. Repeat the process with the second pan. After removing the cake from the oven, let the layers cool before peeling off the parchment paper.

individual lemon poppy seed bundt cakes
with lemon glaze

1/4 cup gluten-free vanilla rice milk

1/4 teaspoon cider vinegar

6 tablespoons water

2 tablespoons ground flaxseed meal

1 1/2 cups Betsy's Baking Mix (see page 88)

2 teaspoons baking powder

1/2 teaspoon salt

1/2 teaspoon xanthan gum

1 cup granulated sugar

1/2 cup organic palm fruit oil shortening

3 tablespoons freshly grated lemon zest (from about 3 lemons)

1 tablespoon poppy seeds

1 recipe Lemon Glaze (recipe follows)

Lemon poppy seed cake was not part of my repertoire until I moved to New York in the late 90's. I used to hang out at a favorite coffee house in my neighborhood and have one piece of cake nearly every day. Naturally, I had to include a gluten-, dairy-, soy-, nut-, and egg-free version in my cookbook.

Makes 6 individual cakes

Preheat the oven to 350°F.. Grease 6 individual 1-cup capacity, mini-Bundt pans with canola oil.

In a small bowl, make "buttermilk" by combining the rice milk and cider vinegar. In another small bowl, combine the water and flaxseed meal and allow to thicken for 3 to 5 minutes. In a large mixing bowl, whisk together the baking mix, baking powder, salt, and xanthan gum.

In the bowl of a stand mixer, cream together the sugar and shortening until they are light and fluffy. Scrape down the sides of the bowl and add the flaxseed mixture and the lemon zest. Beat the mixture for 1 minute and scrape down the sides again.

In 3 additions, add the dry ingredients and "buttermilk" mixture, beginning and ending with the dry ingredients and stirring well after each addition. Fold in the poppy seeds.

Pour the batter into the prepared pans and bake for 20 to 25 minutes, or until the cakes are golden and a toothpick inserted in the centers comes out clean.

Let the cakes cool completely in their pans on a cooling rack. Turn the cakes out of their pans and onto the rack. Spread the glaze on top of the cakes, allowing it to run down the sides.

Store the glazed cakes, covered and refrigerated, for up to 3 days.

you can have your cake and eat it too

lemon glaze

2 cups confectioners' sugar, sifted

2 tablespoons plus 2 teaspoons freshly squeezed lemon juice

Makes enough to glaze 6 individual cakes

In a small bowl, combine the sugar and lemon juice until they are smooth and thin enough to drizzle.

"Fallen cake? Check the internal temperature of your oven and the age of your leavening agent. Either could be the culprit."

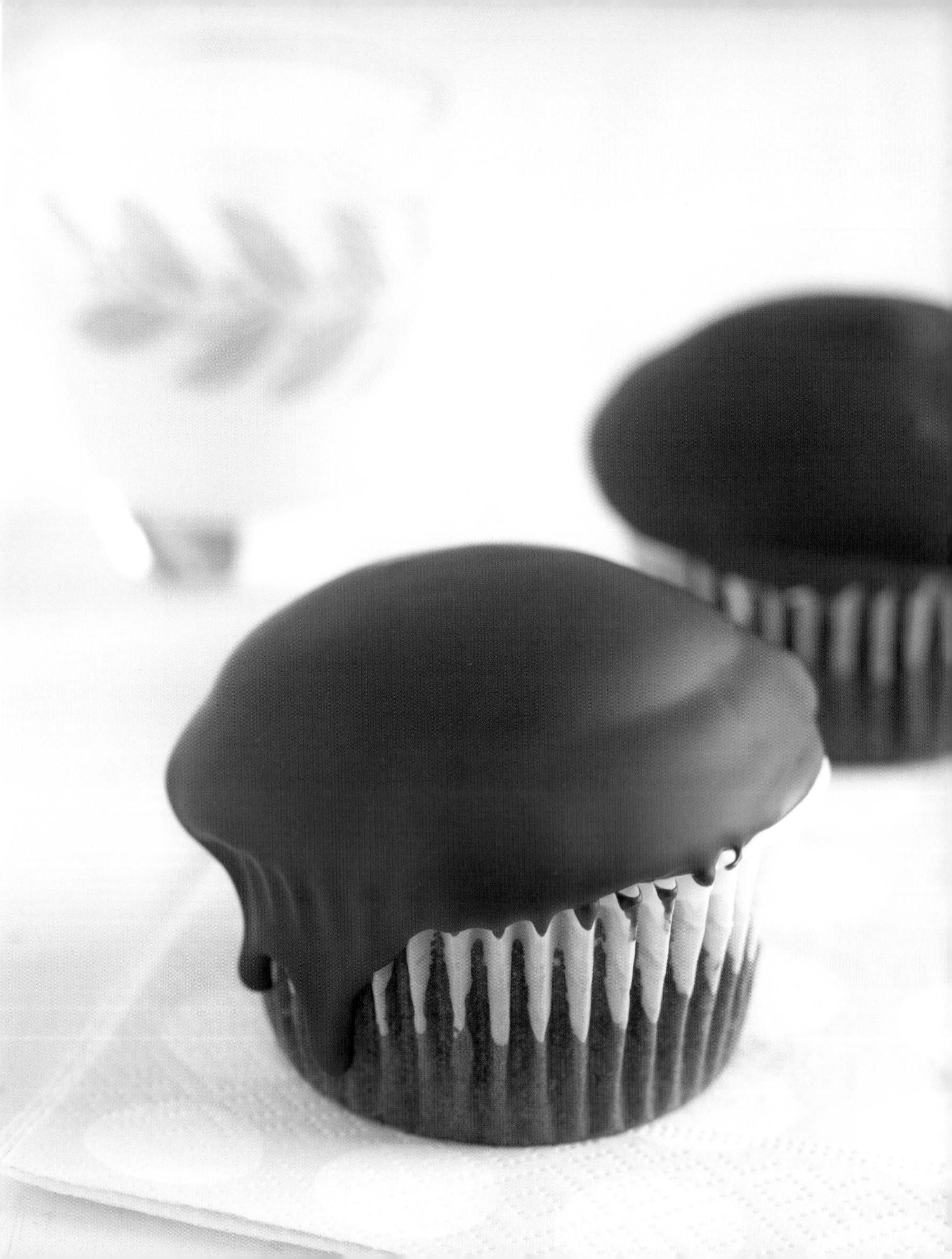

top hats

3 ounces unsweetened
   chocolate, chopped
9 tablespoons water
3 tablespoons ground
   flaxseed meal
2¼ cups Claude's Cake Mix (see
   page 89)
2 teaspoons baking soda
1 teaspoon xanthan gum
½ teaspoon instant espresso
   powder
½ teaspoon salt
½ cup gluten-free vanilla rice
   milk
½ teaspoon cider vinegar
2¼ cups packed dark brown
   sugar
1 cup organic palm fruit oil
   shortening
1 cup boiling water
2 teaspoons vanilla extract
1 recipe Top Hat
   Marshmallow Crème
   (recipe follows)
12 ounces gluten-, soy-, dairy-,
   egg-, and nut-free
   semisweet chocolate chips
1 tablespoon canola oil

After seeing these fancy, chocolate-dipped cupcakes on my favorite cooking show, I just knew that I had to try them. Since my allergies prevented me from trying those made in a local bakery, I set to work to make some that I could enjoy. It was worth the effort and time. These are delicious and always impressive.

Makes 27 cupcakes

Preheat the oven to 350°F. Line 27 cupcake tins with paper liners.

In the top of a double boiler set over simmering water, melt the unsweetened chocolate, stirring until it is smooth. Remove it from the heat and set it aside to cool for 5 minutes.

In a separate small bowl, combine the water and flaxseed meal and allow to thicken for 3 to 5 minutes. Meanwhile, in a separate bowl, combine the cake mix, baking soda, xanthan gum, instant espresso, and salt. In another small bowl, make "buttermilk" by combining the rice milk and the cider vinegar.

In the bowl of a stand mixer, cream together the brown sugar and shortening until light and fluffy. Add the flaxseed mixture, beating well. Stir in the melted chocolate and beat the batter for 1 minute.

Alternately add the dry ingredients and the "buttermilk" mixture to the batter in 3 stages, beginning and ending with the dry ingredients. Slowly stir in the boiling water and the vanilla.

With a ¼-cup measuring cup, pour the batter into the prepared cupcake tins and bake for 17 minutes, or until a toothpick inserted in the centers comes out clean.

Let the cupcakes cool in their tins on cooling racks for 20

CONTINUED ON PAGE 114

you can have your cake and eat it too

top hats

minutes. Remove the cupcakes from the tins and transfer them to the racks to cool completely.

Load a pastry bag fitted with a large tip with the Top Hat Marshmallow Crème and pipe swirls onto the tops of the cooled cupcakes. Place the cupcakes in the refrigerator to set for 2 hours. The frosting should be solid so that it won't melt when it is covered with the melted chocolate.

While the frosted cakes are being refrigerated, combine the chocolate chips and canola oil in the top of a double boiler set over simmering water. Melt the chocolate, stirring to blend. Remove from the heat and allow to cool.

Remove the chilled cupcakes from the refrigerator and dip the mounds of Top Hat Marshmallow Crème in the cooled, melted chocolate mixture. Return the dipped Top Hats to the refrigerator for at least another hour to set.

Store the frosted and dipped cupcakes, covered and refrigerated, for up to 3 days.

how to color **icing:**

Although most of us believe that more is better, it is not always the case with food coloring in icing. I like to use gel colorings because they are more concentrated, yielding a more vibrant color with less food coloring. Remember that decorating and flood icing will dry slightly darker than its wet color.

The best way to color with gel food colorings is to dip a toothpick into the color and add it 1 tiny drop at a time until you have achieved the desired shade. Remember that you can always add more, but you cannot take the color away. Even adding more white icing won't always lighten the color.

A note about natural food colorings: they are a wonderful alternative to food colorings made with corn syrup, but use only a small amount in your recipes. I found out that natural red food coloring, which is made from beets, really tastes like beets. I discovered this when I used it in a red velvet cake and ended up with a beet cake. It was distinctly unappetizing. Thus, when using natural food coloring, use it as sparingly as possible. It does not work in red velvet cake.

top hat marshmallow crème

3 cups Marshmallow Cream
  (see page 129)
1½ cups organic palm fruit oil
  shortening
3 cups confectioners' sugar,
  sifted
2 teaspoons vanilla extract

Makes enough to frost 27 cupcakes

In the bowl of a stand mixer, cream together the marshmallow cream and shortening. Scrape down the sides of the bowl and with the mixer on the lowest setting stir in the confectioners' sugar. Then scrape down the sides again, add the vanilla, and beat the frosting for 2 minutes.

Store the frosting, covered and refrigerated, for up to 5 days.

apple spice cake

9 tablespoons water
3 tablespoons ground flaxseed meal
3 cups Betsy's Baking Mix (see page 88)
2 teaspoons baking soda
1½ teaspoons ground cinnamon
1 teaspoon salt
1 teaspoon xanthan gum
½ teaspoon baking powder
2 cups granulated sugar
1 cup canola oil
1 teaspoon vanilla extract
2 cups peeled shredded apples (from about 3 large McIntosh apples)
¾ cup raisins
1 recipe Maple Glaze (recipe follows)

Given the choice, I would take a spice cake over a chocolate cake any day of the week. The addition of the apples to this recipe makes the cake even moister, and the maple glaze just makes it even tastier.

Serves 8 to 10

Preheat the oven to 350°F. Lightly grease a 10-inch tube pan.

In a small bowl, combine the water and flaxseed meal and allow to thicken for 3 to 5 minutes. In a large bowl, whisk together the baking mix, baking soda, cinnamon, salt, xanthan gum, and baking powder.

In the bowl of a stand mixer, beat the sugar and oil. Scrape down the sides of the bowl and beat in the flaxseed mixture. Scrape down the sides again and stir in the vanilla. Pour in the dry ingredients and stir until moistened. Beat the batter for 2 minutes and scrape down the sides again. Fold in the apples and raisins.

Transfer the batter to the prepared pan and bake for 1½ hours, or until a toothpick inserted near the center comes out clean.

Let the cake cool completely in the pan on a cooling rack. Turn the cake out of the pan and onto a serving plate. Drizzle with about half of the glaze. Let it dry for 30 minutes, then drizzle a second layer of glaze over the cake before serving.

Store the finished cake, tightly wrapped and refrigerated, for up to 3 days.

maple glaze

2 cups confectioners' sugar, sifted
3 tablespoons Grade B maple syrup

Makes enough to glaze one 9-inch Bundt cake

In a small bowl, mix together the sugar and maple syrup until smooth and thin enough to drizzle.

The glaze may be refrigerated in an airtight container for up to 1 week.

"In allergy-free baking, pureed or grated

fruits

and vegetables are great for adding moisture and replacing some fat. "

banana chocolate chip cake

¹/₄ cup gluten-free vanilla rice milk

¹/₄ cup cider vinegar

6 tablespoons water

2 tablespoons ground flaxseed meal

1¹/₄ cups Betsy's Baking Mix (see page 88)

¹/₂ teaspoon baking powder

¹/₂ teaspoon baking soda

¹/₂ teaspoon xanthan gum

¹/₄ teaspoon salt

1 cup granulated sugar

6 tablespoons organic palm fruit oil shortening

2 medium bananas, peeled and mashed (about ³/₄ cup)

1 teaspoon vanilla extract

1 cup gluten-, soy-, dairy-, egg-, and nut-free semisweet chocolate chips

1 recipe Sunflower Seed Buttercream (recipe follows)

This cake is the brainchild of the pastry chef at Good Enough to Eat, a neighborhood favorite on the Upper West Side. Until I learned of my food allergies, I was a fixture at the restaurant every Thursday evening so that I could sample their famous banana chocolate chip cake with peanut butter icing. The last time I ran into Carrie Levin, the restaurant owner, I told her I couldn't wait to make a version of it for this book. The addition of the Sunflower Seed Buttercream is the crowning glory of this recipe.

Serves 8 to 10

Preheat the oven to 350°F. Grease two 8-inch round cake pans with canola oil, line the bottoms of the pans with parchment paper, and then lightly grease the parchment paper.

In a small cup or bowl, make "buttermilk" by combining the rice milk and cider vinegar. In another small bowl or cup, combine the water and flaxseed meal and allow to thicken for 3 to 5 minutes. In a medium bowl, whisk together the baking mix, baking powder, baking soda, xanthan gum, and salt.

In the bowl of a stand mixer, cream together the sugar and shortening. Add the mashed bananas and beat until the batter is smooth. Beat in the flaxseed mixture and the vanilla. Stir in the dry ingredients, alternately adding the buttermilk and dry ingredients and ending with the dry, until they are thoroughly combined, and then fold in the chocolate chips.

Pour the batter into the prepared pans and bake for 25 minutes. Then turn the heat down to 325°F and bake the cakes for another 8 minutes, or until a toothpick inserted in the centers comes out clean.

CONTINUED ON PAGE 122

you can have your **cake** and eat it too

CONTINUED FROM PAGE 120

banana chocolate chip cake

Let the cakes cool completely in their pans on a cooling rack. Turn the cakes out of the pans and remove the parchment paper. Frost the top of each cake layer with the frosting. Transfer 1 layer to a serving plate, and then set the other cake layer on top. Frost the sides of the cake.

Store the frosted cake, covered and refrigerated, for up to 3 days.

sunflower seed buttercream

1 recipe Vanilla Buttercream Frosting (see page 93)
1 cup organic palm fruit oil shortening
$^2/_3$ cup smooth sunflower seed butter
$1^1/_2$ cups confectioners' sugar, sifted
$^1/_2$ teaspoon vanilla extract
$^1/_4$ teaspoon salt

Sounds weird, I know, but sunflower seed butter is an amazing alternative to peanut butter. They taste amazingly similar. You can use this as a delicious frosting on top of the Banana Chocolate Chip Cake, on chocolate cake, or on anything that tastes great with peanut butter, or spread it on top of anything chocolate. You will be amazed that there is no peanut butter in it.

Makes enough to frost and fill one 8-inch layer cake or 24 cupcakes or fill 12 sandwich cookies

Combine the buttercream frosting, shortening, and sunflower seed butter in the bowl of a stand mixer. Beat until fluffy and the sunflower seed butter is evenly mixed in. Scrape down the sides of the bowl, then stir in the sugar, vanilla, and salt. Beat the frosting for another 2 minutes.

The frosting may be refrigerated in an airtight container for up to 1 week, or frozen for up to 3 months.

pineapple upside-down cake

¼ cup plus ⅓ cup organic
  palm fruit oil shortening
½ cup packed dark brown
  sugar
  One 14-ounce can
  pineapple rings packed in
  syrup, drained
7 maraschino cherries
⅔ cup gluten-free vanilla rice
  milk
¾ teaspoon cider vinegar
3 tablespoons water
1 tablespoon ground
  flaxseed meal
1½ cups Betsy's Baking Mix
  (see page 88)
2 teaspoons baking powder
½ teaspoon baking soda
½ teaspoon salt
½ teaspoon xanthan gum
1 cup granulated sugar
1 teaspoon vanilla extract

Pineapple upside-down cake strikes me as such a throwback to the 50's, and perhaps it's no mistake that it is my father-in-law's favorite birthday cake. For some reason, I find it so intriguing that it can be baked in a cast-iron skillet, and I love the decorative lattice work created by the rings of pineapple on the top of the cake.

Serves 6 to 8

Preheat the oven to 350°F.

In a heavy 10-inch cast-iron skillet or 10-inch round cake pan, melt ¼ cup of the shortening over medium heat. Remove from the heat and sprinkle the brown sugar over the melted shortening. Arrange the drained pineapple in a circular pattern over the bottom of the pan, placing 1 cherry in the middle of each pineapple ring.

In a small bowl, make "buttermilk" by combining the rice milk and cider vinegar. In a small cup, combine the water and flaxseed meal and allow to thicken for 3 to 5 minutes.

In the bowl of a stand mixer, mix together the baking mix, baking powder, baking soda, salt, and xanthan gum. Add the remaining ⅓ cup of shortening, the "buttermilk" mixture, granulated sugar, and vanilla and beat for 2 minutes. Scrape down the sides of the bowl, add the flaxseed mixture and beat until thoroughly combined.

Pour the batter on top of the pineapple in the cast-iron skillet. Bake for about 30 minutes, or until the cake is golden and a toothpick inserted in the center comes out clean. Remove it from the oven and immediately turn the cake upside down on a serving platter, leaving the pan in place on top of the cake for a few minutes while the brown sugar runs down the sides of the cake. Allow the cake to cool completely before serving.

Store the cooled cake, covered and refrigerated, for up to 3 days.

you can have your **cake** and eat it too

caramel cake

6 tablespoons water
2 tablespoons ground
   flaxseed meal
2¼ cups Betsy's Baking Mix
   (see page 88)
1 cup granulated sugar
1 tablespoon baking powder
1 teaspoon salt
1 teaspoon xanthan gum
½ teaspoon baking soda
½ cup organic palm fruit oil
   shortening
⅓ cup Caramel Sauce (see
   page 176), cooled but not
   solidified
1 teaspoon vanilla extract
1 recipe Caramel
   Buttercream Frosting
   (recipe follows)

When I started this book, I surveyed all of my friends and family for inspiration. One of my friends immediately suggested caramel cake, which is, apparently, even more Southern than a red velvet cake. This is a very dense cake that is especially delicious with Caramel Buttercream Frosting.

Serves 8 to 10

Preheat the oven to 350°F. Lightly grease two 8-inch round cake pans with canola oil, line the bottoms of the pans with parchment paper, and then lightly grease the parchment paper with canola oil.

In a small bowl, combine the water and flaxseed meal and allow to thicken for 3 to 5 minutes.

In the bowl of a stand mixer, gently mix the baking mix, sugar, baking powder, salt, xanthan gum, and baking soda. Add the shortening and caramel sauce and beat for 2 minutes. Scrape down the sides of the bowl with a rubber spatula. Add the flaxseed mixture and the vanilla and beat again for another 2 minutes. The batter will be very thick.

Spoon the batter into the prepared pans and bake for 30 to 35 minutes, or until the cakes are golden and a toothpick inserted in the centers comes out clean.

Let the cakes cool in their pans on a cooling rack for 40 minutes. Turn the cake layers out of their pans and onto the racks and cool completely before removing the parchment paper.

Frost the top of each cake layer with the frosting. Transfer 1 cake layer to a serving plate, and then set the other cake layer on top. Frost the sides of the cake.

Store the frosted cake, covered and refrigerated, for up to 3 days.

caramel buttercream frosting

2 cups Vanilla Buttercream
   Frosting (see page 93)
1 cup Caramel Sauce (see
   page 176), cooled but not
   solidified

Makes enough to fill and frost one 8-inch layer cake or 24 cupcakes

Combine the Vanilla Buttercream Frosting and the Caramel Sauce in the bowl of a stand mixer fitted with the paddle attachment and beat for 2 minutes, or until the frosting is thick and fluffy.

The frosting should be used immediately.

"When whipped, gelatin, water, and simple **syrup** become thick, just like marshmallow and become similar to 7-minute frosting."

marshmallow cream

½ cup cold water
3 packages unflavored gelatin
2 cups Lyle's Golden Syrup
2 cups confectioners' sugar, sifted
1½ teaspoons vanilla extract
½ teaspoon salt

My marshmallow cream reminds me of ice cream sundaes and my mother's homemade fudge. It also reminds me of fluffernutter sandwiches and just eating spoonfuls of it out of that jar with the red lid and blue and white label. Basically, it reminds me of all the things that are now my dietary taboos. Finding out that it was made with eggs devastated me, but I'm relieved to know that I can make an alternative. I recommend using Lyle's Golden syrup instead of corn syrup as a natural alternative, but this will yield an off-white color. If this bothers you, then feel free to use corn syrup instead. Note that this frosting base is neither vegan nor kosher, but there is an appropriate alternative frosting on page 97.

Makes 4 cups

In a small saucepan, add the cold water and sprinkle the gelatin over it. Let stand for 5 minutes. Add the Lyle's Golden Syrup and heat the mixture over medium heat, stirring constantly, for 4 to 5 minutes, or just until the gelatin is completely dissolved.

Pour the gelatin and syrup mixture into the bowl of a stand mixer and beat for 3 minutes on medium speed, and then for 12 minutes at medium-high speed. The mixture will become thick, fluffy, and very sticky, just like commercial marshmallow cream.

Stir in the confectioners' sugar, vanilla, and salt until combined, then beat on medium-high for another 2 minutes. Scrape down the sides of the bowl and beat for another minute. The longer it sits at room temperature, the stickier (more like a marshmallow) it will become.

Store, covered and refrigerated, for up to 3 days. Or store in an airtight container in the freezer for up to 3 months. To defrost the cream, just place it in the refrigerator for several hours, and then let it sit at room temperature for another hour.

you can have your cake and eat it too

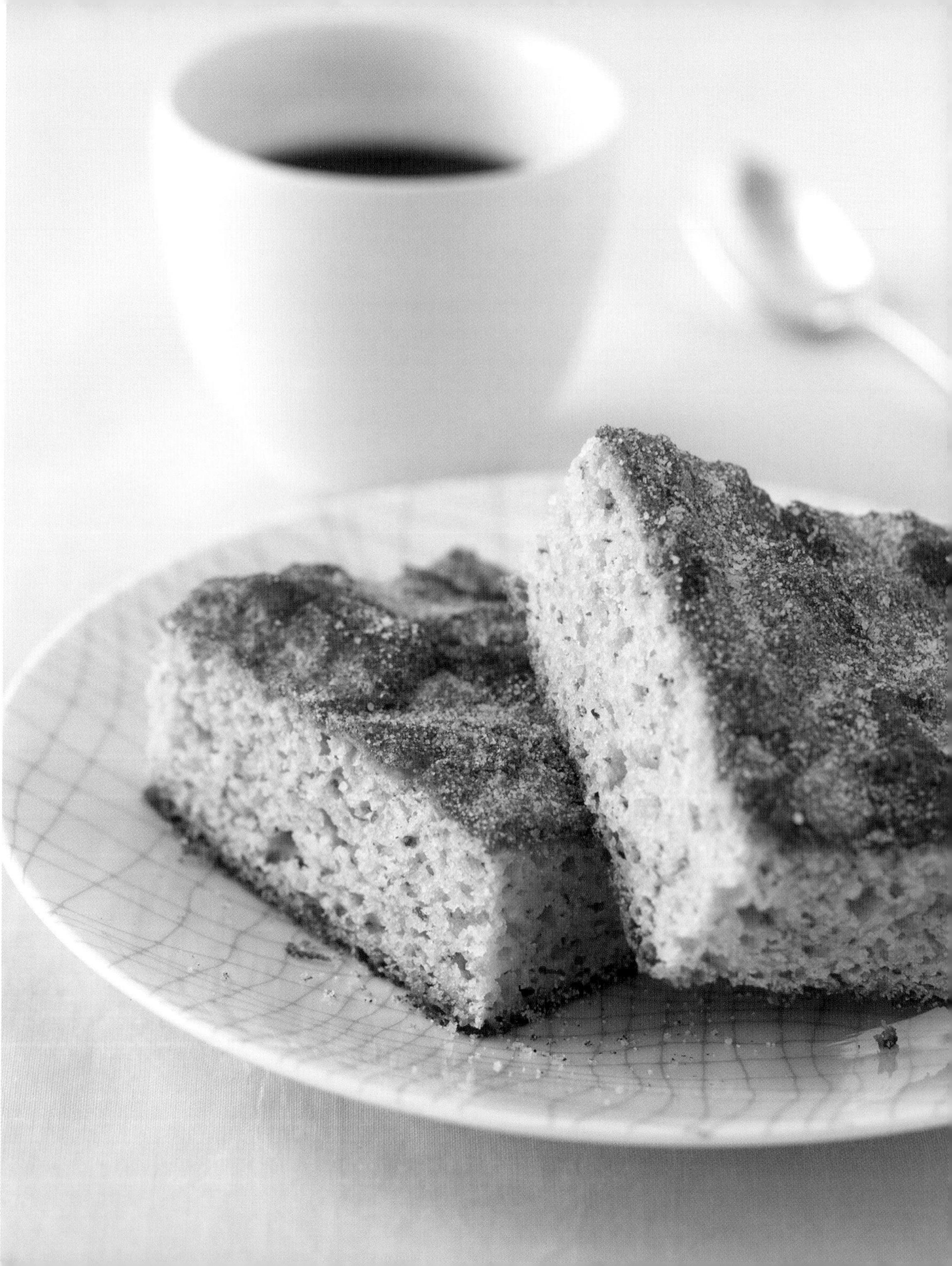

super quick cinnamon coffee cake

3 tablespoons water
1 tablespoon ground
  flaxseed meal
$\frac{1}{2}$ cup gluten-free vanilla rice
  milk
$\frac{1}{2}$ teaspoon cider vinegar
$1\frac{3}{4}$ cups Betsy's Baking Mix
  (see page 88)
1 cup plus 1 tablespoon
  granulated sugar
2 teaspoons baking powder
$\frac{1}{2}$ teaspoon baking soda
$\frac{1}{2}$ teaspoon xanthan gum
$\frac{1}{4}$ cup organic palm fruit oil
  shortening
$\frac{1}{2}$ teaspoon vanilla extract
$1\frac{1}{2}$ teaspoons ground
  cinnamon

This is such a simple, unbelievably moist cake and great to whip up for a casual brunch or for an afternoon tea break.

Serves 8

Preheat the oven to 375°F. Lightly grease an 8-inch square baking pan with canola oil.

In a small bowl, combine the water and flaxseed meal and allow to thicken for at least 3 to 5 minutes. In another small bowl, make "buttermilk" by combining the rice milk and cider vinegar.

In a large bowl, mix together the baking mix, 1 cup of the sugar, the baking powder, baking soda, and xanthan gum. Using a pastry blender or 2 knives, blend in the shortening until the mixture resembles coarse meal. Then blend in the flaxseed mixture, the "buttermilk" mixture, and the vanilla.

Pour the batter into the prepared pan and smooth it out. Mix the remaining 1 tablespoon of sugar and the cinnamon in a small bowl, then sprinkle the cinnamon sugar over the top of the batter.

Bake the cake for 20 to 25 minutes, or until the top is golden and a toothpick inserted in the center comes out clean. Let the cake cool completely in the pan on a cooling rack before slicing it and serving.

Store the cooled cake, tightly wrapped in an airtight container and refrigerated, for up to 3 days.

gingerbread cake

2 cups Betsy's Baking Mix
(see page 88)
1½ teaspoons baking soda
1½ teaspoons ground ginger
1 teaspoon xanthan gum
½ teaspoon salt
¼ teaspoon plus 1 tablespoon
ground cinnamon
½ cup well-shaken
unsweetened coconut
milk (not light)
½ teaspoon cider vinegar
3 tablespoons water
1 tablespoon ground
flaxseed meal
1 cup molasses
⅓ cup organic palm fruit oil
shortening
½ cup raisins
3 tablespoons granulated
sugar

I remember the first time I made gingerbread. I had no idea at the time that gingerbread came in any other form than little cut out cookies, so imagine my surprise when I poured this into a pan and voilà, a cake appeared in the oven. This tastes great plain, but it's especially yummy with Vanilla Buttercream Frosting (see page 93) on top.

Serves 8

Preheat the oven to 325°F. Lightly grease a Bundt pan with canola oil.

In a medium mixing bowl, whisk together the baking mix, baking soda, ginger, xanthan gum, salt, and ¼ teaspoon of the cinnamon. In a small bowl, make "buttermilk" by combining the coconut milk and cider vinegar. In another small bowl, combine the water and flaxseed meal and allow to thicken for 3 to 5 minutes.

In a large saucepan, heat the molasses and shortening over low heat until lukewarm. With a hand mixer, beat in the "buttermilk" mixture and the thickened flaxseed mixture. Stir in the dry ingredients and fold in the raisins.

Pour half of the mixture into the prepared pan and smooth with a knife. Sprinkle the batter with the sugar and the remaining 1 tablespoon of cinnamon, then top with the remaining batter. Bake for 55 minutes, or until a toothpick inserted near the center comes out clean. Cool the cake completely in the pan on a cooling rack for 40 minutes. Turn it out onto a serving plate and serve.

Store the finished cake, covered and refrigerated, for up to 3 days.

" **Ginger has healing properties and is great for morning sickness.**

Cinnamon

is believed to lower cholesterol. "

cola cake

6 tablespoons water
2 tablespoons ground
   flaxseed meal
$\frac{1}{2}$ cup gluten-free vanilla rice
   milk
$\frac{1}{2}$ teaspoon cider vinegar
2 cups Betsy's Baking Mix
   (see page 88)
2 cups granulated sugar
1 teaspoon xanthan gum
$1\frac{1}{2}$ cups gluten-free and
   egg-free mini
   marshmallows
1 cup cola
$\frac{1}{2}$ cup canola oil
$\frac{1}{2}$ cup organic palm fruit oil
   shortening
3 tablespoons unsweetened
   cocoa powder
1 teaspoon vanilla extract
1 teaspoon baking soda
1 recipe Chocolate Cola Icing
   (recipe follows)

This is a Southern favorite that few Northerners have ever heard of, much less tasted. It is so fudgy and rich. No one ever guesses that cola is in it.

Serves 12

Preheat the oven to 350°F. Lightly grease a 9 x 13-inch baking pan with canola oil.

In a small bowl, combine the water and flaxseed meal and allow to thicken for 3 to 5 minutes. In another small bowl, make "buttermilk" by combining the rice milk and cider vinegar. In a large mixing bowl, sift together the baking mix and sugar. Add the xanthan gum and thoroughly combine. Stir in the mini marshmallows.

In a medium saucepan, combine the cola, oil, shortening, and cocoa powder. Cook over medium heat, stirring, until it boils. Pour the chocolate mixture into the baking mix in the large bowl and stir to thoroughly combine.

Add the flaxseed mixture and the vanilla to the batter and stir well. Add the baking soda to the "buttermilk" mixture and then add it to the batter. Stir well until the batter is completely smooth.

Pour the batter into the prepared pan and bake for 45 minutes, or until a toothpick inserted in the center comes out clean. Remove the cake from the oven and immediately spread the icing over the hot cake and let it cool completely in the pan on a cooling rack.

Store the iced cake, covered and refrigerated, for up to 3 days.

chocolate cola icing

¾ pound confectioners' sugar
6 tablespoons cola
⅓ cup organic palm fruit oil shortening
3 tablespoons unsweetened cocoa powder
1 teaspoon vanilla extract

I love this frosting because it's quick and can go on a cake immediately when it comes out of the oven. For an impatient, time-pressed person like me, it's a great solution in a time crunch.

Makes enough to ice one 9 x 13-inch sheet cake

Sift the confectioners' sugar into a large mixing bowl. Combine the cola, shortening, and cocoa powder in a saucepan. Over medium heat, stir the mixture until it is smooth and then bring it to a boil. Remove from the heat and pour over the confectioners' sugar. Stir until it is smooth, then stir in the vanilla. The icing must be used immediately.

moist marble pound cake

½ cup well-shaken unsweetened coconut milk (not light)
½ teaspoon cider vinegar
1½ cups Betsy's Baking Mix (see page 88)
1½ teaspoons baking powder
½ teaspoon baking soda
½ teaspoon salt
½ teaspoon xanthan gum
6 tablespoons water
2 tablespoons ground flaxseed meal
¾ cup granulated sugar
½ cup organic palm fruit oil shortening
1 teaspoon vanilla extract
2 teaspoons unsweetened cocoa powder

I find that my eldest daughter can never make up her mind about whether she likes chocolate or vanilla better. This way, she doesn't have to decide. She can have both chocolate and vanilla at the same time in one yummy pound cake.

Serves 6 to 8

Preheat the oven to 350°F. Lightly grease a 9 x 5-inch loaf pan with canola oil.

In a small bowl, make "buttermilk" by combining the coconut milk and cider vinegar. In a large bowl, whisk together the baking mix, baking powder, baking soda, salt, and xanthan gum. In another small bowl, combine the water and flaxseed meal and allow to thicken for 3 to 5 minutes.

In the bowl of a stand mixer, cream together the sugar and shortening. Scrape down the sides of the bowl and beat in the thickened flaxseed mixture and the vanilla. Scrape down the sides of the bowl again. In 3 additions, alternately stir in the dry ingredients and the "buttermilk" mixture, starting and ending with the dry ingredients. Mix ½ cup of the batter in a separate bowl with the cocoa powder. Then spread the vanilla batter into the prepared pan. Drop dollops of the chocolate batter on top of the vanilla batter. Using a wooden skewer or a knife, make a decorative swirl in the batter.

Bake the cake for 25 to 30 minutes, or until the top is golden and a toothpick inserted in the center comes out clean. Let the cake cool completely in the pan on a cooling rack before turning out onto a serving platter and slicing.

Store the completely cooled cake, tightly wrapped and refrigerated, for up to 5 days, or freeze for up to 3 months.

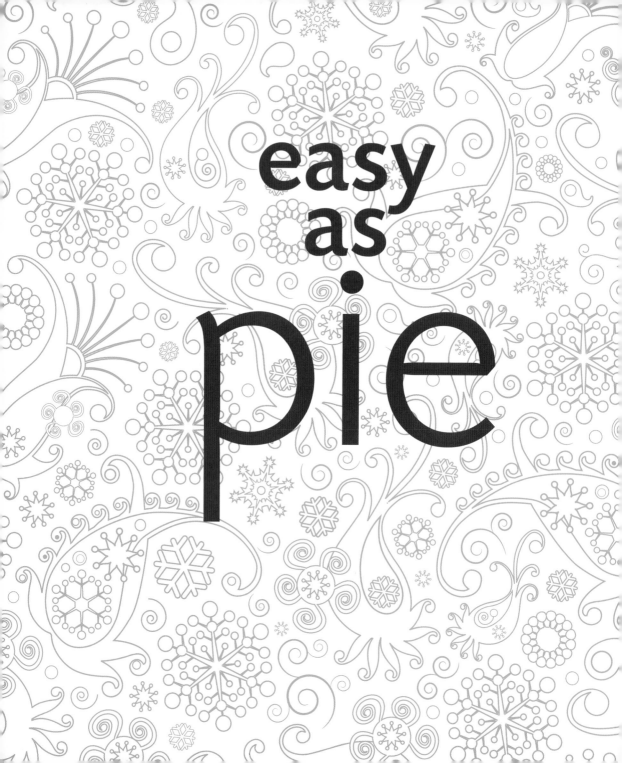

easy as

as

pie

It is a rare weekend that I call my mother and find her not making pies. Often-times she is making ten or twenty for a charity function, and other times she's just using up the last of the apples that she handpicked from the neighbor's apple trees. When my mom makes a crust, it is always tender and flakey, and it takes her just minutes to make a pie dough that is perfect.

At the start of this project, I felt that I had a high standard to meet, so I made my mother test all of the pie recipes in this section. Fortunately, the garbanzo flour lends depth of flavor to the crust, while the potato starch and tapioca flour make the crust delicate and flakey. Thus the pie crust that I came up with is really tasty. I cook down all of the fruit fillings so that they are juicy and sweet, but never soupy.

When my husband tasted these pies, he told me that he thought that I should quit the cookie business and devote myself, exclusively, to pies.

cookie crust

1½ cups rice flour (white or brown)
¼ cup packed light brown sugar
1 teaspoon salt
¼ teaspoon ground cinnamon
5 tablespoons liquefied organic refined coconut oil (stir before measuring if not completely liquid)
3 tablespoons honey
2 teaspoons vanilla extract

A graham cracker crust is, to me, an essential part of American baking. While it was difficult to replicate both the taste and texture of a real graham crust, I believe this is as close of a replication as one can come. It's delicious and offers all of the same taste elements as a regular cookie crust, and the best part is that there is no baking involved.

Makes one 9-inch pie crust

In a medium bowl, combine the rice flour, brown sugar, salt, and cinnamon and blend with your fingers until thoroughly mixed and all of the large lumps are gone; the mixture will be grainy. Stir in the oil, honey, and vanilla until thoroughly combined.

Turn the mixture out into a 9-inch pie plate or tart pan with removable sides and press it into the pan with your fingers or the back of a soup spoon. Refrigerate the crust, uncovered, for at least 30 minutes, then fill with the filling of your choice.

Store the finished crust, refrigerated, until ready to use or for up to 2 days.

chocolate cookie crust

1¼ cups rice flour (white or brown)
½ cup unsweetened cocoa powder
¼ cup packed dark brown sugar
1 teaspoon instant espresso powder
½ teaspoon salt
5 tablespoons liquefied organic refined coconut oil (stir before measuring if not completely liquid)
3 tablespoons agave syrup
3 tablespoons Grade B maple syrup

This recipe is so useful. It can be used as a crust for a bar cookie or as a crust for a fruity tart. The possibilities are endless, and again, no-bake, so super quick.

Makes one 9-inch pie crust

In a large bowl, whisk together the rice flour, cocoa powder, brown sugar, espresso powder, and salt. Add the coconut oil, agave syrup, and maple syrup and mix with a fork until the dry mixture is moistened.

Press the crust into a 9-inch tart pan with removable sides and chill for at least 30 minutes before filling it.

Store the finished crust, refrigerated, until ready to use or for up to 2 days.

pumpkin pie

1 recipe Single Pie Crust (see page 144), chilled but not rolled out
Two 15-ounce cans solid pack pureed pumpkin
1 cup liquefied organic refined coconut oil (stir before measuring if not completely liquid)
²/₃ cup packed dark brown sugar
1 tablespoon vanilla extract
2 teaspoons ground cinnamon
1 teaspoon salt
½ teaspoon ground allspice
½ teaspoon ground ginger
Pinch of freshly ground black pepper

The inspiration for this pie recipe came from my first Thanksgiving in New York City. My employers were kind enough to include me in their plans, and they baked the most delicious pumpkin pie that I have ever tasted. This is an egg-free, unbaked adaptation of it.

Serves 6 to 8

Preheat the oven to 375°F.

Roll out the chilled crust between 2 sheets of parchment paper until it is large enough to fit into a 9-inch deep-dish pie plate. Remove the parchment paper and press the crust into the pie plate. Crimp the edges and prick the crust all over with a fork.

Lightly grease a sheet of aluminum foil with canola oil, then press it down over the crust. Place pie weights on top of the foil. Bake the crust for 25 minutes, or until it is golden brown. Remove the crust from the oven and then remove the pie weights and foil. Allow the crust to cool completely.

Place the pumpkin puree, oil, brown sugar, vanilla, cinnamon, salt, allspice, ginger, and black pepper in the pitcher of a high-speed blender. Blend on high for 1 minute, scrape down the sides of the pitcher, then blend again for another minute. Pour the "custard" batter into the cooled crust, then let it chill for 3 hours, or until set, before serving. Because of the low melting point of the coconut oil, be sure to keep the pie refrigerated until just before serving and right after cutting it.

Store the pie, covered and refrigerated, for up to 2 days.

single pie crust

5 tablespoons cold water
2 cups Betsy's Baking Mix
   (see page 88)
1 teaspoon salt
1 teaspoon xanthan gum
²/₃ cup organic palm fruit oil
   shortening, chilled

Pie crust is notoriously difficult to make, but the beauty of this one is that it is simple and very forgiving. If the crust cracks once it is in the pan, just press it back together. If some of the crust comes off while crimping, just pinch it back on. The flours and the shortening lend themselves to flakiness, so you will not be disappointed.

Makes one single 9-inch pie crust

Measure the water into a liquid measuring cup and place it in the freezer just while you are measuring and mixing the other ingredients.

In a large bowl, whisk together the baking mix, salt, and xanthan gum. Then cut in the chilled shortening with a pastry cutter (do not use your hands). There should be lumps the size of peas in the dough; it is very important not to overmix the dough. Add the water a small amount at a time, tossing lightly with a fork to mix just until the dough begins to come together.

Dump the dough out onto plastic wrap and wrap tightly. Press the dough into a ball, then flatten it into a disk. Double wrap the dough and let it chill for at least 30 minutes.

Remove the chilled dough from the refrigerator and roll it out between 2 sheets of parchment paper (or on a floured pastry cloth), rolling from the middle in one direction only and turning an eighth of a turn with each roll, until the dough is $1/8$ inch thick and a large enough circle to fit a 9-inch pie plate.

Remove the parchment paper and press the dough into a 9-inch pie plate. If the dough cracks, just press it back together with your fingers. Crimp the edges and use according to your recipe's instructions.

Store the unbaked pie crust, tightly wrapped and frozen, for up to 2 months.

helpful tip: This may also be used as a double pie crust, but I find that it doesn't work as well by just doubling the ingredients. Make 2 separate recipes for the double pie crust.

conversions for
convection baking:

All of the recipes in this book were tested using a conventional oven. Convection ovens circulate air in the oven, cooking the food inside more evenly and faster than in a conventional oven. I didn't base the recipes on convection, because not everyone has one. In fact, I didn't have a convection oven at home until this year. However, if you have a convection oven and would prefer to bake with the convection on, here are some tips for doing so. If you are baking something that is supposed to bake for less than 15 minutes, then leave the baking time as the recipe states, but reduce the oven temperature by 25% to 30%. If the recipe calls for a longer baking time than 15 minutes, then keep the oven temperature as stated in the recipe but reduce the baking time by 25% to 30%.

rhubarb galette

1 **pound rhubarb, leaves removed and stalks cut into 1-inch chunks**
1 **cup granulated sugar**
2 **tablespoons cornstarch**
1 **recipe Single Pie Crust (see page 144), chilled but not rolled out**

Galette is just a fancy word for a free-form pie, so don't be daunted by this twist on an old favorite. This galette is best served immediately so that the crust doesn't have a chance to get soggy. I like to put it in the oven just before guests arrive for coffee so that it is cool enough to eat it just as they are walking in the door.

Serves 4 to 6

Preheat the oven to 400°F. Line a cookie sheet with parchment paper.

In a large sauté pan, combine the rhubarb, sugar, and cornstarch and cook over medium-high heat for 5 to 7 minutes, or until the rhubarb has released its juices and the juices have begun to thicken.

While the rhubarb is cooking down, roll the pie crust between 2 sheets of parchment paper into a 12-inch round. Remove the parchment paper from the crust and place the crust on the parchment-lined baking sheet.

When the rhubarb juices have begun to thicken, remove the rhubarb mixture from the heat and pile it onto the center of the prepared crust, leaving a 2-inch border of crust around the filling. Using the parchment paper as an aid, fold the crust edges up around the rhubarb mixture, then bake for 35 to 40 minutes, or until the pie crust is golden and the rhubarb mixture is bubbly.

Let the galette cool for 20 minutes, cut into wedges, and serve. The galette is best served immediately.

lemon ice box pie

1 recipe Cookie Crust (see page 140)

2 cups confectioners' sugar, sifted

$^3/_4$ cup liquefied organic refined coconut oil (stir before measuring if not completely liquid)

$^1/_2$ cup packed freshly grated lemon zest (from about 5 large lemons)

$^1/_4$ cup freshly squeezed lemon juice

I really love this pie. It is so tart, so cool, and so creamy, and the lemon flavor is so powerfully refreshing. It is the perfect, light finish to a summery meal. Just be sure not to leave it in the heat as coconut oil has such a low melting point that it will melt very quickly.

Serves 8

Press the cookie crust into a 9-inch tart pan with removable sides and let it chill for at least 30 minutes.

Combine the sugar, coconut oil, lemon zest, and lemon juice in the pitcher of a blender. Blend on high for 30 seconds, scrape down the sides, and blend again for another 30 seconds.

Pour the lemon mixture into the prepared cookie crust, place the pie in the refrigerator, and chill for at least 4 hours before serving. Keep refrigerated until just before serving. Remove from the tart pan just before serving and cut into wedges.

Store the pie, covered and refrigerated, for up to 3 days.

rustic pear tarte tatin

2 tablespoons organic palm fruit oil shortening

2 pounds Bosc pears (4 to 5 pears), peeled, cored, and quartered

¾ cup granulated sugar

2 tablespoons cornstarch

1 recipe Single Pie Crust (see page 144), chilled but not rolled out

This recipe reminds me of my life in Paris after college. It's what the French would consider a simple dessert, and they are right, it is easy to make. I find that it's best to cook the pears in a large paella pan—it's large enough to hold all of them. Then bake them in a glass pie plate so that you can see when they are done.

Serves 8

Position the oven rack in the center of the oven and preheat the oven to 400°F.

Melt the shortening in a large skillet over medium-high heat. Add the pears, sugar, and cornstarch and cook, stirring occasionally to make sure the pears and sugar do not stick to the pan, for 15 minutes or until the pears release their juices and soften. The juices will have begun to thicken. Transfer the pear mixture to an ungreased 9-inch glass pie dish. Unlike a traditional tarte Tatin, you may arrange the pears in any way you choose. I like to pile them in.

Roll out the chilled pie crust between 2 sheets of parchment paper so that it is just larger than the diameter of the pie dish. Remove the parchment paper and drape the crust over the pear mixture, then fold the crust edges around the pears and tuck them into the dish. Place the pie dish on a cookie sheet and transfer to the center rack of the oven. Bake for 30 to 35 minutes, or until the crust is golden brown and the pear mixture is bubbly.

Cool the tarte Tatin in the pie dish on a cooling rack. As it cools, the filling will firm, making it easier to slice and serve straight from the pie dish. This dessert tastes best the day it is made and served either at room temperature or slightly warm.

apple pie

½ cup granulated sugar
2 tablespoons cornstarch
2 teaspoons ground cinnamon
½ teaspoon salt
6 Golden Delicious apples, peeled, cored, and cut into chunks (about 2 cups)
2 recipes Single Pie Crust (see page 144), chilled but not rolled out
2 tablespoons superfine sugar

Given that apple pie is an American staple, this book didn't feel complete without a recipe for one.

Serves 8

Preheat the oven to 400°F.

In a large bowl, stir together the granulated sugar, cornstarch, cinnamon, and salt. Add the apples and toss to coat. In a large sauté pan, cook the apple mixture over medium heat, stirring frequently, for 5 to 8 minutes, or until the apples have released their juices and the juices have begun to thicken.

While the apples are cooking, roll out each crust separately between 2 sheets of parchment paper until it is large enough to leave a 1-inch overhang on the pie plate. Remove the parchment paper from one crust and press the crust into the pie plate. Pour the cooked apple mixture into the prepared pie plate. Remove the parchment paper from the second crust and drape the crust over the pie. Crimp the edges of the pie crusts together, then cut several vents in the top crust. Mist the top crust with just a tiny amount of water and sprinkle the top with the superfine sugar.

Bake the pie for 40 minutes, or until the crust is golden and the apple mixture is bubbly; if the edges of the pie begin to brown too quickly, cover them with foil for the remainder of the baking time. Let the pie cool completely in the pan on a cooling rack before cutting it.

Store the pie, covered and refrigerated, for up to 3 days. This pie also freezes very well after it has been baked and completely cooled. Just wrap it tightly with plastic wrap, then freeze for up to 3 months. Easily defrost this pie by removing it from the freezer and letting it sit at room temperature for 3 hours.

key lime pie

1 recipe Cookie Crust (see page 140)
5 very ripe avocados
1 cup sifted confectioners' sugar
$\frac{1}{2}$ cup freshly squeezed lime juice (from about 6 limes)
$\frac{1}{3}$ cup freshly grated lime zest
$\frac{1}{4}$ cup liquefied organic refined coconut oil (stir before measuring if not completely liquid)
1 teaspoon vanilla extract
$\frac{1}{4}$ teaspoon salt
Twists of lime peel, for garnish

My husband used to own an ice cream shop, so when he brought home the Vita-Mix blender that they used to make fruit smoothies, I nearly went weak in the knees. It blends so well that I immediately set out to make one of his favorite desserts as a thank you. Instead of an eggy custard-filled key lime pie, I created something that I could also enjoy with avocado as the very pleasant, green base. Feel free to use a regular blender for your version.

Serves 8

Press the cookie crust into a 9-inch tart pan with removable sides and chill for at least 30 minutes.

Peel and seed the avocados. Scoop the flesh into the pitcher of a blender. Add the sugar, lime juice, zest, oil, vanilla, and salt and blend on high speed until thoroughly pureed and completely smooth, stopping occasionally to scrape down the sides of the pitcher.

Pour the lime filling into the prepared cookie crust and smooth it with a spatula. Cover the pie with plastic wrap, then press the plastic wrap directly onto the surface of the filling to prevent the filling from discoloring. Chill the pie for 4 hours, keeping it refrigerated until just before serving. The filling will be set, but not completely solid. Remove the pie from the tart pan, slice, and garnish with lime twists to serve.

Store the finished pie, covered and refrigerated, for up to 3 days.

plum tart

1 recipe Single Pie Crust (see page 144), chilled but not rolled out
1½ pounds red plums, pitted and quartered
¾ cup granulated sugar
1 tablespoon cornstarch

Out on the East End of Long Island, we have the most succulent, juiciest plums at the beginning of August. I love to stop by a fruit stand, stock up, then make one of these for an afternoon treat for my family.

Serves 8

Preheat the oven to 400°F.

Roll out the pie crust between 2 sheets of parchment paper until it is large enough to leave a 1-inch overhang on the tart pan. Remove the parchment paper and press the crust into a 9-inch tart pan with removable sides. Trim the edges of the pie crust to fit the pan, then prick the crust all over with a fork. Lightly grease a sheet of aluminum foil with canola oil, then press it down over the crust. Bake for 12 minutes, or until the crust is golden brown. Remove from the oven, uncover the crust, and allow it to cool on a cooling rack.

While the pie crust is baking, combine the plums, sugar, and cornstarch in a sauté pan over medium-high heat and cook until the juices have released and begun to thicken, about 10 minutes. Pour the plum mixture into the pie crust and return to the oven for 30 minutes, or until the plum mixture is bubbly and the crust is golden.

Store the finished tart, covered and refrigerated, for up to 2 days.

how to roll out cookie
or pie dough:

This is one of my favorite tips, and I learned it when I was interning for a well-known Manhattan wedding cake designer. This makes it so easy to clean up after rolling out the dough, and with this method, there is no way that the dough can stick to the countertop or the rolling pin.

  Place the ball of dough between two sheets of parchment, roll from the middle, turning the circle $\frac{1}{4}$ turn clockwise after each roll. This keeps the dough from sticking, makes it easier to move the dough to a pie tin, keeps the dough in a circle, and makes cleanup super easy.

extraordinary
extras

These goodies are all of the yummy treats that can be served at the end of the meal or for an afternoon treat but don't fall into a discreet cake, pie, or cookie category. Rustic cobblers, homespun candies, rich sauces, and creamy puddings are at the heart of this section. Most of the desserts are simple and fairly quick. Whip up something for a coffee break and serve it warm, or make the fudge and keep it frozen and on hand for when you need a chocolate fix. Either way, I am sure you will enjoy all of them.

individual blackberry cobblers

1 cup plus 2 tablespoons Betsy's Baking Mix (see page 88)
$\frac{1}{2}$ cup granulated sugar
1 teaspoon baking powder
$\frac{1}{2}$ teaspoon baking soda
$\frac{1}{2}$ teaspoon xanthan gum
$\frac{1}{2}$ cup gluten-free vanilla rice milk
$\frac{1}{2}$ teaspoon cider vinegar
18 ounces fresh blackberries
1 tablespoon cornstarch
3 tablespoons organic palm fruit oil shortening

I love making individual desserts for a dinner party, since I find no one feels quite as guilty when they've eaten a discreet serving as opposed to a heaping helping of one big cobbler.

Serves 4

Preheat the oven to 400°F and place 4 six-ounce ramekins on a baking sheet.

In a small bowl, whisk together the baking mix, $\frac{1}{4}$ cup of the sugar, the baking powder, baking soda, and xanthan gum. In another small bowl, make "buttermilk" by combining the rice milk and cider vinegar.

Combine the blackberries, cornstarch, and the remaining $\frac{1}{4}$ cup of sugar in a sauté pan and cook over medium-high heat for 5 to 7 minutes, stirring occasionally, or until the berry juices begin to thicken. Spoon the berry mixture into the ramekins.

Cut the shortening into the flour mixture until the mixture resembles a coarse meal, then pour in the "buttermilk" mixture. Stir the dough until it is thoroughly combined, then, with an ice cream scoop, scoop the batter onto the top of the berry-filled ramekins.

Bake for 20 minutes, or until the cobbler tops are golden brown and the berries are bubbling. Remove from the oven and allow to cool slightly. These are wonderful served warm and they are best eaten the day they are made.

super easy dark chocolate fudge

3³/₄ cups unsweetened cocoa
      powder
3 cups agave syrup
1¹/₂ cups organic refined
      coconut oil (stir before
      measuring if not
      completely liquid)
³/₄ teaspoon instant espresso
      powder
¹/₂ teaspoon salt

I love fudge, but it can be tricky to make. Cook it too long and it is dry, not long enough, and it won't harden. So, I came up with this as a very foolproof way to make fudge. This also makes an excellent frosting for cupcakes if you don't chill it, and instead, immediately spread it on top of the cakes and then chill them. This fudge is made with coconut oil, so it will melt very quickly if left at room temperature. Just leave it in the freezer and pull out a piece as necessary.

Serves 16

Grease an 8-inch square baking pan with a little canola oil.

In a large bowl, stir together the cocoa powder, agave syrup, coconut oil, espresso powder, and salt until thoroughly combined and smooth. Spread into the prepared pan and freeze for 2 to 3 hours, or until firm. Cut into squares.

Store, covered and frozen, for up to 3 months or until gone.

helpful tip: The fudge can be used as a ganache frosting. Simply spread the fudge over cooled cupcakes while it is at room temperature, then refrigerate the cupcakes until just before serving. Do not freeze the fudge if using it as a frosting.

chocolate pots de crème

2 very ripe avocados
$^3/_4$ cup unsweetened cocoa powder
$^2/_3$ cup Grade B maple syrup
$^1/_4$ cup agave syrup
1 teaspoon vanilla extract
$^1/_2$ teaspoon instant espresso powder
$^1/_2$ teaspoon salt

This is an incredibly rich, no-cook pudding, and your children will never, ever guess there is something green in it. Use very ripe avocados to make it smoother and creamier. These can be garnished with mint, berries, candied orange peels, sprinkles, or bananas.

Makes about 6 servings

Peel and seed the avocados. Scoop the avocado flesh into the pitcher of a blender. Add the cocoa powder, maple syrup, agave syrup, vanilla, espresso powder, and salt. Puree on high speed until thoroughly combined and completely smooth, stopping frequently to scrape down the sides of the pitcher. Pour the pudding into individual 5- or 6-ounce ramekins, chill, and serve.

Store the puddings, covered and refrigerated, for up to 2 days.

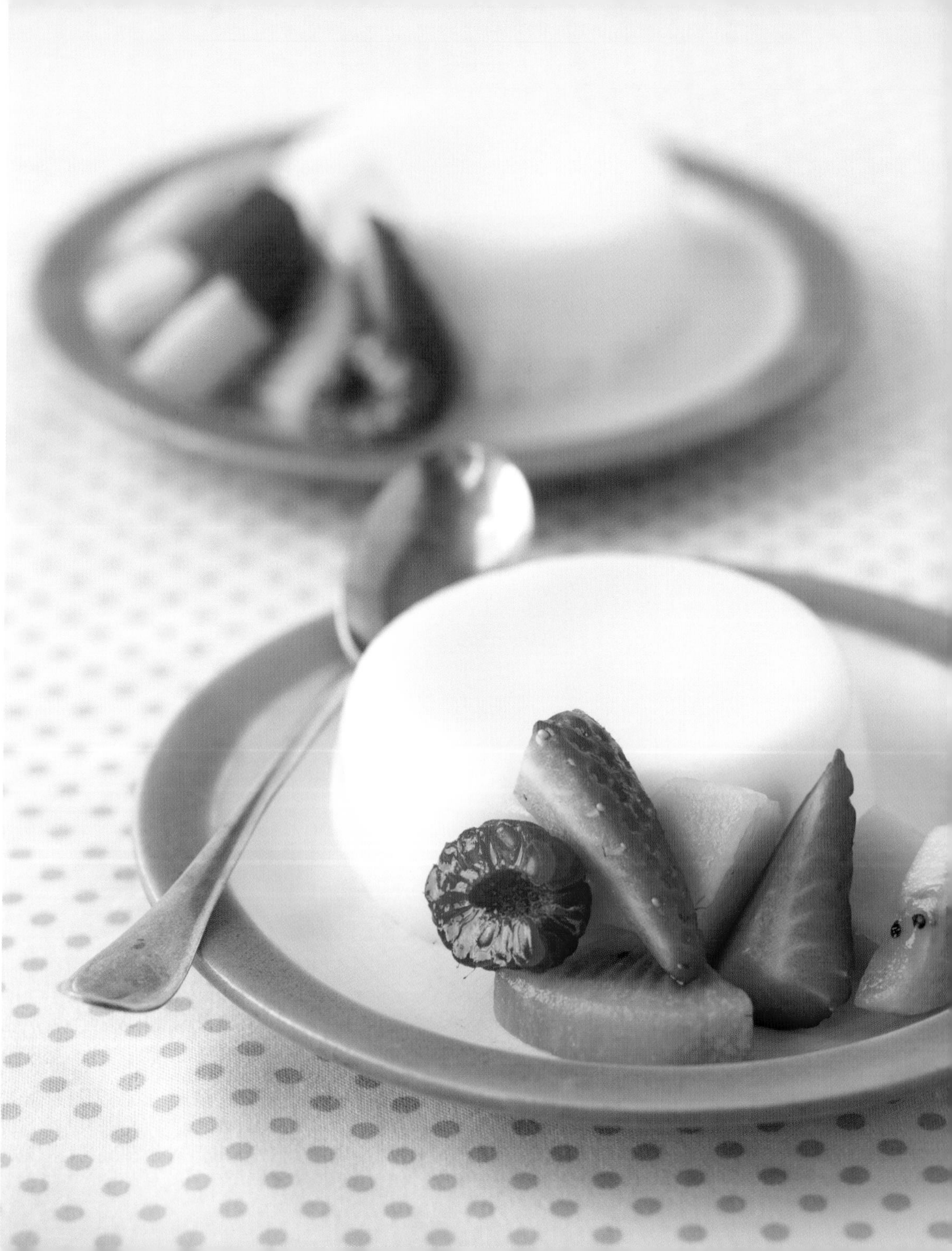

coconut panna cotta

6 14-ounce chilled cans
   unsweetened coconut
   milk (not light),
   well-chilled and unshaken
1 package unflavored gelatin
½ cup granulated sugar
1½ teaspoons vanilla extract
   Seasonal fruit, for serving

Smooth and creamy, richer than pudding, these panna cottas are the perfect end to any meal. I skim the creamy solids that rise to the top of chilled coconut milk to simulate rich, heavy dairy cream in this recipe. Just don't shake the cans of coconut milk before chilling so that the creamy solids rise to the top, making them easier to skim. Canned "coconut cream" that is in most supermarkets is not appropriate for this recipe as it is just thickened, corn syrup-sweetened coconut milk. This panna cotta only works with the all natural regular, not light, coconut milk.

Makes 6 servings

Skim 3 cups of the coconut "cream" from the top of the chilled coconut milk in the cans (do not shake the cans in order to keep the milk and cream separate).

Pour 1 cup of the skimmed coconut milk solids into a saucepan and sprinkle the gelatin over the top. Let sit for 5 minutes. Then, with the heat on low, stir the mixture constantly until the gelatin has dissolved. Pour in the remaining 2 cups of skimmed coconut milk solids, then stir in the sugar and vanilla. Continue cooking the mixture over low heat, stirring, until the sugar is completely dissolved. Remove from the heat and pour into 6 individual, 5- or 6-ounce ramekins.

Refrigerate for at least 4 hours, but preferably overnight. Remove from the refrigerator and garnish them with seasonal fruit before serving.

To unmold, dip the ramekins in warm water for 1 minute, then turn over, and tap gently onto a plate.

Store unmolded panna cottas, covered and refrigerated, for up to 2 days.

lazy daisy rice pudding

4 cups gluten-free vanilla rice
   milk
$^3/_4$ cup extra long-grain white
   rice
$^1/_2$ cup raisins
$^1/_3$ cup granulated sugar
$^1/_2$ teaspoon ground cinnamon
$^1/_4$ teaspoon salt

To me, there is no comfort food more comforting than a bowl of creamy, cinnamony rice pudding. Not having to stir it or even tend to it as it is cooking makes it even better. In essence, this really is the perfect recipe.

Serves 4

Mix all of the ingredients in a slow cooker, then cover and cook on high for $3^1/_2$ hours, or until the rice is tender and the mixture is thick and creamy. Stir the pudding, then let it cool slightly before serving. The pudding may be served warm or cold.

Store the cooled rice pudding, covered and refrigerated, for up to 5 days.

how to soften
brown sugar:

To soften hardened brown sugar, place $\frac{1}{2}$ pound of the sugar in a bowl and cover the top of the bowl with wet paper towels. Cover the bowl tightly with aluminum foil and let the sugar sit overnight. Break up the sugar in the morning and use it immediately.

cool mint patties

1 pound confectioners' sugar, sifted
5 tablespoons organic palm fruit oil shortening
2½ teaspoons peppermint extract
½ teaspoon vanilla extract
6 tablespoons Lyle's Golden Syrup
12 ounces gluten-, soy-, dairy-, egg-, and nut-free semisweet chocolate chips

When I was growing up, York Peppermint Patties were my brother's favorite candies. I could never understand when given a choice between a Peppermint Pattie or a Milky Way bar, why he always went for the Pattie, but as an adult, I get it. The peppermint is bracing while the chocolate is so rich. Given the choice now, I'd take a Pattie, too.

Makes about 3 dozen patties

In a large bowl, combine the sugar, 3 tablespoons of the shortening, and the peppermint and vanilla extracts. Add the Lyle's Golden Syrup and mix thoroughly with a large spoon.

With a very small ice cream scoop or tablespoon measure, scoop out the dough and roll it into balls. Place on a wax paper–lined baking sheet and chill for 30 minutes. Remove from the refrigerator and press the balls with the bottom of a glass to form ¼-inch-thick patties. Return the patties to the baking sheet and chill for another 30 minutes.

After the patties have chilled, combine the chocolate and the remaining 2 tablespoons of shortening in the top of a double boiler set over simmering water. Stir until the chocolate is completely melted. Allow the chocolate mixture to cool for 10 minutes. Dip the patties in the chocolate mixture so they are completely coated, then place the patties on wax paper–lined baking sheets. Place the baking sheets in the refrigerator and let the peppermint patties dry for at least an hour before serving.

Store the completely dried patties, covered and refrigerated, for up to 1 week.

chocolate syrup

¼ cup Grade B maple syrup
¼ cup unsweetened cocoa
  powder
2 tablespoons water
1 tablespoon agave syrup
⅛ teaspoon salt

This is such a versatile dessert topping. It tastes great drizzled over a piece of unfrosted vanilla cake or marble cake, poured over any commercial allergen-free ice cream that fits your dietary restrictions, or used with rice milk for either ice cold chocolate milk or hot cocoa.

Makes about ½ cup

Stir all of the ingredients together in a small saucepan until they are thoroughly combined. Bring the mixture to a boil over low heat, stirring constantly. Let the syrup cool slightly before spooning it over desserts or combining it with rice milk for a nice treat. This tastes great either slightly warm like hot fudge or at room temperature.

Store the chocolate syrup, covered and refrigerated, for up to 3 days. To reheat: Pour the syrup into a saucepan and, stirring constantly, warm over low heat or until just warmed.

helpful tip: To make chocolate milk or hot chocolate, pour 1 to 2 tablespoons of the chocolate sauce into 8 ounces rice milk. Serve the chocolate milk cold, or for hot chocolate, just heat the drink until it is your preferred temperature and top with gluten- and egg-free marshmallows.

homemade applesauce

1½ pounds McIntosh apples
    (about 4 large apples),
    peeled, cored, and halved
7 tablespoons water
3 tablespoons granulated
    sugar
½ teaspoon ground cinnamon

We have an apple tree in our yard, and I hate to waste any of the precious apples that the deer are kind enough to leave us in the early fall. This recipe is a great way to use them up. My youngest daughter cannot get enough of this applesauce.

Serves 6

Preheat the oven to 400°F and line a baking sheet with parchment paper. Place the apples on the prepared sheet and roast for 30 minutes. The apples will soften and turn a golden brown.

Being careful because the apples will be hot, transfer the roasted apples to the pitcher of a blender. Add the water, sugar, and cinnamon. Blend on high speed until smooth, then pour the applesauce into individual bowls. Refrigerate until cold and serve.

Store the applesauce, covered and refrigerated, for up to 5 days.

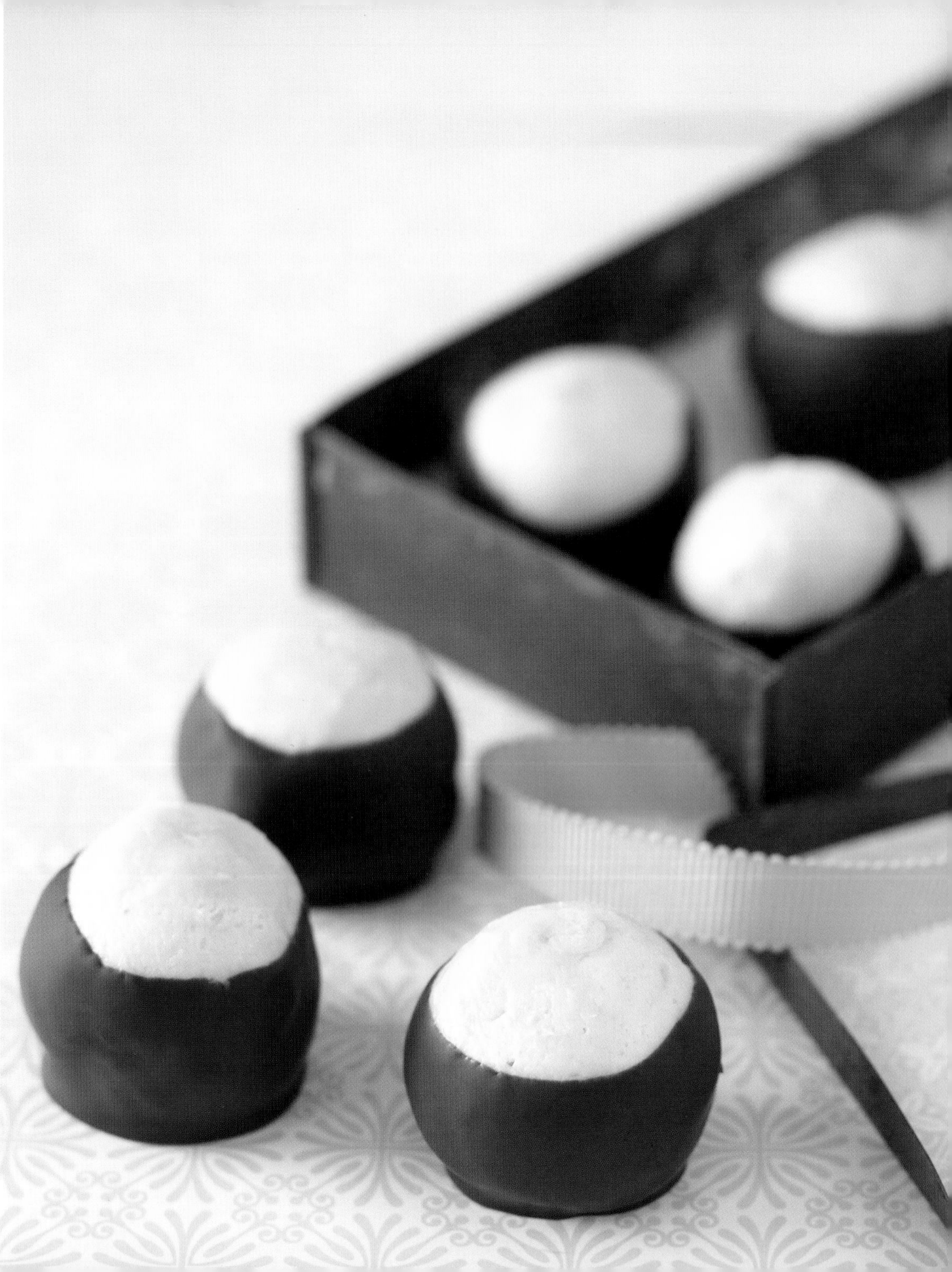

buckeyes

2 cups Vanilla Buttercream Frosting (see page 93)
2 tablespoons plus 2 teaspoons sunflower seed butter
  Confectioners' sugar, for coating hands
24 ounces gluten-, soy-, dairy-, egg-, and nut-free semisweet chocolate chips
2 tablespoons canola oil

There is not a self-respecting Ohioan around who isn't familiar with these special candies. We make them at the holidays, and they always amaze those who have never before tried them. I never thought they would be possible to make without peanut butter, but my husband swears that he likes these better than the real thing! These are best served in the cooler months.

Makes 36 buckeyes

Line 2 baking sheets with parchment paper.

In the bowl of a stand mixer, beat the frosting and the sunflower seed butter together until they are light and fluffy, and then refrigerate the mixture for 30 minutes.

After the buttercream mixture has chilled slightly, coat your hands with confectioners' sugar (to keep the buttercream from sticking), scoop the frosting mixture by tablespoonfuls, and roll them between your hands into balls. Place the balls on the prepared baking sheets and refrigerate for at least 1 hour, or until they are solid.

Melt the chocolate and oil together in the top of a double boiler set over simmering water, stirring occasionally, until smooth. Let the chocolate mixture cool for 5 minutes. With a toothpick, dip the balls into the chocolate, leaving a little circle of brown frosting visible at the top. Place the buckeyes on the parchment-lined sheets to dry. Refrigerate until the chocolate is hard and shiny.

Store the buckeyes, covered and refrigerated, for up to 1 week.

fudgsicles

1/4 cup superfine sugar

3 tablespoons unsweetened cocoa powder

2 cups gluten-free vanilla rice milk

1/8 teaspoon vanilla extract

In the summer, my mother always kept a box of Fudgsicles and a box of Creamsicles in the freezer for a special treat. On one of the hottest days of the year, I knew I needed to create a new recipe, but I couldn't bear the thought of baking something. In that heat, the memories of cold, creamy Fudgsicles came to me, and I had to make my own version immediately.

Serves 6

In a small bowl, mix together the sugar and cocoa powder.

In a medium saucepan, heat the rice milk over medium heat until small bubbles appear just at the edges of the pan. When the bubbles form, remove the saucepan from the heat and pour 1/3 cup of the warm rice milk into the cocoa powder mixture. Stir until a thick, smooth paste forms, then pour the paste back into the rest of the warm rice milk and stir until the chocolate is uniformly combined and completely smooth. Let the chocolate milk cool slightly.

Pour the slightly cooled chocolate milk into popsicle molds and freeze for at least 3 hours, or until firm, before serving.

Keep frozen for up to 3 months.

bananas foster

4   bananas, peeled
2   teaspoons organic refined
     coconut oil (stir before
     measuring if not
     completely liquid) or
     canola oil
$\frac{1}{2}$ teaspoon ground cinnamon
1   recipe Butterscotch Sauce
     (see page 176), warm
4   slices Caramel Cake (see
     page 126), unfrosted

When I was growing up, there was only one 5-star restaurant in Ohio. It was called the Maisonette, and we used to go there whenever we went to the opera. I always looked forward to the end of the meal when somebody inevitably ordered bananas Foster, because it was prepared at the table. Of course, at the restaurant, it was flambéed and served over vanilla ice cream. This recipe is not, but it is equally as tasty. I like to serve it over unfrosted cake or ice cream.

Serves 4

Slice the bananas in half lengthwise, then cut them in half again, so that you have quarters.

Heat the oil in a large sauté pan over medium heat and add the bananas. Cook the bananas until they are soft and start to brown all over. Remove the bananas from the heat.

In a small bowl, stir the cinnamon into the warm butterscotch sauce, then pour the sauce over the sautéed bananas.

Spoon the bananas and sauce over unfrosted cake or commercially prepared ice cream that fits your dietary restrictions.

peach crisp

Topping

3/4 cup garbanzo bean flour
3/4 cup packed light brown
 sugar
1/4 teaspoon xanthan gum
1/2 cup organic palm fruit oil
 shortening
1 cup gluten-free rolled oats

Filling

1/4 cup granulated sugar
2 tablespoons cornstarch
1/2 teaspoon ground cinnamon
2 pounds frozen sliced
 peaches, thawed and
 well-drained, or about 4
 large fresh peaches, pitted
 and cut into 1/2-inch-thick
 slices

This is something so simple to make with frozen peaches, and it's even more delicious when peaches are in season.

Serves 6

Preheat the oven to 375°F.

To make the topping, in a medium bowl, mix the garbanzo flour, brown sugar, and xanthan gum. Using a fork or your fingers, cut in the shortening until the mixture resembles a coarse meal. Mix in the oats, then place the mixture in the freezer while you are preparing the peach filling.

To make the filling, in a small bowl, combine the sugar, cornstarch, and cinnamon. Place the peaches in a large nonstick sauté pan and sprinkle the cornstarch mixture over them. Cook over medium-high heat, stirring often, for 5 to 7 minutes, or until the peach juice begins to thicken. Remove the pan from the heat and pour the peaches into a 2-quart casserole dish.

Sprinkle the topping over the peaches and bake for 20 minutes, or until the topping is golden and the peaches are bubbly. Place on a rack to cool. This tastes great at room temperature or slightly warm.

Store the crisp, covered and refrigerated, for up to 2 days.

butterscotch or caramel sauce

1 tablespoon agar
¾ cup cold gluten-free vanilla rice milk
¼ cup organic refined coconut oil (stir before measuring if not completely liquid)
1 cup packed dark brown sugar
1 tablespoon vanilla extract, optional
1 teaspoon salt, optional

This recipe is somewhat of a "key recipe." I use it as a topping, as an important component to three frostings, and as an essential ingredient for brownies and cake. Make sure to have all of your ingredients measured and at your fingertips. The sugar will not wait and can burn very easily.

Makes 1 cup

Sprinkle the agar over the cold rice milk in a small saucepan. Let it sit for 5 minutes, then set the saucepan over medium heat and bring the mixture just to a boil. Reduce the heat and simmer for another 3 to 5 minutes, stirring to dissolve the agar completely.

Meanwhile, heat the oil in a medium sauté pan over medium heat and stir in the sugar until moistened. Cook, stirring, for 4 to 5 minutes, or until the sugar turns a dark golden brown and just begins to liquefy. Remove the pan from the heat; if you wait too long, the sugar will scorch and stick to the pan. When you remove the pan from the heat, immediately stir in the rice milk mixture and whisk until it thickens slightly. For butterscotch, stir in the vanilla and salt, then let the sauce cool slightly but not until it solidifies. (The agar will act like gelatin to thicken the completely cooled sauce.) If you are making caramel sauce, omit the vanilla and salt.

Store the sauce, covered and refrigerated, for up to 5 days. When you are ready to use the sauce again, whisk it over low heat until it is warm and liquefied again.

"Brown sugar has more molasses than white sugar and is less sweet."

index

allergy-free **desserts**

186